6/94

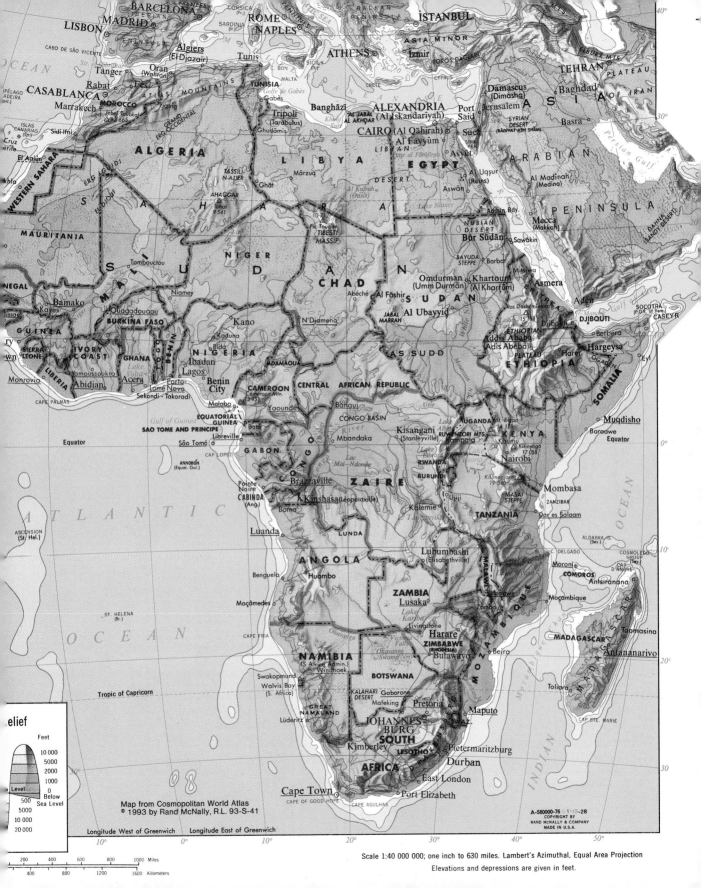

Enchantment of the World

BOTSWANA

By Jason Lauré

Consultant for Botswana: Alice Gordon Apley, Ph.D. Candidate in Anthropology, New York University, New York City

Consultant for Reading: Robert L. Hillerich, Ph.D., Professor Emeritus, Bowling Green State University, Bowling Green, Ohio; Consultant, Pinellas County Schools, Florida

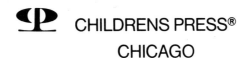
CHILDRENS PRESS®

CHICAGO

Gathering mushrooms growing on a huge termite mound in Moremi Wildlife Reserve

Project Editor: Mary Reidy
Design: Margrit Fiddle

Library of Congress Cataloging-in-Publication Data

Lauré, Jason.
  Botswana / by Jason Lauré.
    p.   cm. — (Enchantment of the world)
  Includes index.
  Summary: Describes the geography, climate, history, economy, culture, and people of Botswana.
  ISBN 0-516-02616-X
  1. Botswana—Juvenile literature. [1. Botswana.]
I. Title. II. Series.
DT2437.L38   1993   93-753
968.83—dc20   CIP
                                               AC

Picture Acknowledgments
The Bettmann Archive: 17 (right), 21
CIDA Photo: © **Bruce Paton,** 64 (bottom left and bottom right)
© **John Elk III:** © **Wezelman,** 67 (left), 69 (top left), 70 (left), 87 (right), 88 (top)
GEOImagery: © **Erwin C. Bud Nielsen,** 67 (right), 98 (right), 103
H. Armstrong Roberts: © **J. Moss,** 114
Lauré Communications: 15, 17 (left), 23 (left), 25 (right), 29 (2 photos), 30, 38, 39 (2 photos), 68, 82 (left), 91, 109 (right); © **Jason Lauré,** 4, 7 (left), 12, 19, 43, 45 (2 photos), 46 (2 photos), 47 (2 photos), 48, 53, 54, 55 (right), 59 (2 photos), 62 (left), 64 (top), 69 (right), 70 (right), 71 (2 photos), 73 (2 photos), 76, 77 (2 photos), 80 (right), 83, 86 (right), 87 (left), 88 (bottom left & right), 89, 90 (2 photos), 92 (right), 93 (3 photos), 94 (bottom right), 96 (2 photos), 99 (2 photos), 100 (center left & bottom right), 105, 109 (left), 110, 111, 113; © **Izak Barnard,** 5; © **Anthony Bannister/ABPL,** 8 (right), 55 (left), 62 (right), 79, 80 (left), 86 (left); © **Timothy Livesedge/ABPL,** 49; © **Lorna Stanton/ABPL,** 11; © **Argus,** 34, 82 (right); © **AAC,** 50
North Wind Picture Archives: 18
Photri: 7 (right), 8 (left), 91 (right), 94 (bottom left), 98 (left)
Reuters/Bettmann: 72
Root Resources: © **Mrs. Jane H. Kriete,** 92 (left); **Stan Osolinski,** 100 (bottom left); © **Mary & Lloyd McCarthy,** 100 (center right)
Tom Stack & Associates: © **F. S. Mitchell,** 75; © **Kevin Schafer & Martha Hill,** 104
Stock Montage: 23 (right), 25 (left)
Tony Stone Images: © **Chris Harvey, Cover;** © **Roy Giles,** 94 (top)
SuperStock International, Inc.: © **The Holton Collection, Cover Inset;** © **S. Gould,** 10; © **World Photo Service,** 66; © **Holton Collection,** 100 (top)
UPI/Bettmann: 41
Valan: © **Aubrey Lang,** 69 (bottom left), 106
Len W. Meents: Maps on 92, 103
Courtesy Flag Research Center, Winchester, Massachusetts 01890: Flag on back cover
Cover: Gemsboks, large antelopes, in the Kalahari landscape
Cover Inset: Women in a Herero village

Impalas at the Okavango Delta

TABLE OF CONTENTS

Chapter 1

THE NATION OF

BOTSWANA

THE PEOPLE

Botswana is a country whose people are mainly from one ethnic group—the Tswana. However, through the years, the Tswana broke into eight main clans, all related to one another. Sometimes one group of families would leave an area because of disagreements with the *kgosi*, the local chief. More often it was because the group had become too large or because there was a drought. They would move to other areas where they could find enough grazing and water for their cattle, and fertile land where they could grow enough food.

All these people speak the same language, Setswana. In the Setswana language, changes in meaning are indicated by changing the first syllable of a word or adding a prefix. For example, the people in the country of Botswana are known as *Batswana*; the language they speak is *Setswana*. When a word is made plural, the change also is shown in the prefix: the word for one chief is kgosi; the plural is *dikgosi*.

The eight clans of Batswana are the Bangwato, Bakwena, Bangwaketse, Batawana, Bakgatla, Batlokwa, Bamalete, and Barolong. Seretse Khama, Botswana's first president, and his

San (left) live in the Kalahari Desert and
many Herero (right) live in the northwest.

ancestors were Bangwato. The Bamalete are not of Tswana origin,
but through the years of living among the Tswana took on their
culture, customs, and language.

There are about 1.3 million people living in Botswana. Most of
them belong to the eight Tswana clans. There also are small
groups of people belonging to other cultures who make their
home here, including about twenty-five thousand Herero people
who live in the northwest and an estimated fifty thousand people
called *San*, also known as the Bushmen of the Kalahari. The San
are descendants of the earliest people who lived in Botswana.
They once lived throughout southern Africa, but were pushed
into the less desirable parts of the land by the arrival of Bantu and
European people. Eventually, the San were forced to live in the
Kalahari Desert.

ENVIRONMENT

One word sums up the hope and dilemma of Botswana, and that word is pula. *Pula* means "rain" in Setswana. Rain is so scarce and so important in Botswana that the word pula was taken as the name of the country's currency. The word also appears on the country's coat of arms. A common form of greeting is to wish another person "good pula."

GEOGRAPHY

Botswana is a landlocked country in the southern part of Africa. It is wedged between Namibia to the west and north, South Africa to the south and east, and Zimbabwe to the northeast. Botswana just touches Zambia to the north. Botswana is a large country, 231,805 square miles (600,376 square kilometers), a little smaller than Texas and a little larger than France. About three-quarters of the land area is taken up by the Kalahari Desert, called the "great thirst land" by the people who live there. Most of the country is a plateau that averages about 3,300 feet (1,006 meters) in altitude. Most of the people live along the hilly eastern portion of the country, the most fertile part.

Rivers mark long stretches of Botswana's boundaries. The northeast border is formed by the Chobe and Shashi rivers, the southeast by the Limpopo, the southwest by the Nossob, and the southern border by the Molopo. The border with Namibia to the west and the northwest is just a line on the map. This is where the Kalahari Desert sprawls over the landscape, covering much of Botswana and the eastern part of Namibia. In the 1990s, harsh drought caused the Limpopo to dry up completely.

Opposite page: A few goats graze on the scrub bushes of the Kalahari. The sun rises over the Chobe River in Chobe National Park (inset).

During the rainy season, the Okavango River is filled with water.

LAND AND WATER

Water rules Botswana's land and its people, coming and going in dramatic seasonal changes. There is very little permanent surface water in Botswana. People store water by building dams. They also dig for water that is found in underground reservoirs. During the rainy season, the great Okavango River gushes with water. Over the months that follow, virtually all of this water evaporates. Some makes its way to the Boteti River, which only flows during part of the year. One river, the Savuti, dried up during a great drought in 1982 and has remained dry ever since. Lake Ngami is rarely filled with water. It was dry throughout most of the 1980s.

CLIMATE

January is the hottest month of the year in Botswana. Temperatures range between 86 degrees Fahrenheit (30 degrees Celsius) and 94 degrees Fahrenheit (34.4 degrees Celsius). July is the coldest month, reaching 33 degrees Fahrenheit (0.5 degree

The Kalahari Desert has sparse vegetation.

Celsius) in the Kalahari and 47 degrees Fahrenheit (8.3 degrees Celsius) in the extreme north. Rainfall has become more and more uncertain. Droughts did occur in the past, but lately they have come more often, with fewer good years in between, and they last longer. In the early 1980s, a severe drought across southern Africa killed crops and livestock and forced people off the land. It eased in the late 1980s, only to be followed by another drought that continued into the 1990s. The same loss of crops and livestock was repeated.

KALAHARI

The Kalahari is a desert that looks different from most. It covers much of Botswana and extends into neighboring Namibia and South Africa. It is called a desert because it has no permanent source of surface water, but much of it is covered by sparse grasses. Sand dunes cover only a small portion of the southwestern Kalahari. Great portions are set aside as game reserves, but they are difficult to visit because of the severe weather and lack of paved roads and other facilities for visitors.

Chapter 2

SETTLING BOTSWANA

ANCIENT HISTORY

About two million years ago the ancestors of early humans lived on the land known today as Botswana. Ancestors of the San are believed to have lived in the Kalahari for at least twenty-five thousand to fifty thousand years. They were the first people to live here. Through rock paintings and stone tools that have been found, we know a bit about how these people lived. They were hunters and gatherers who lived off the land.

TSODILO HILLS

In the northwest corner of Botswana lie the Tsodilo Hills, home to thirty-five hundred rock paintings. The paintings are thought to be at least two thousand to three thousand years old, clear proof of the San's presence in the region. Anthropologists believe that there once were much older paintings, reflecting the even more ancient San who lived here as long as twenty-five thousand to thirty thousand years ago. The existing paintings depict the animals the San hunted: eland (a large antelope), ostrich, giraffe, and sometimes mythical animals that play a role in the legends.

Opposite page: The rock paintings in the Tsodilo Hills are thought to be at least two to three thousand years old.

MIGRATIONS

The rest of the people who live in Botswana are descended from those who migrated here more recently. The main thrust of migration is thought to have taken place in the middle of the thirteenth century. Negroid people called Bantu moved south out of Central Africa and settled in the area south of the Limpopo River, today known as the Transvaal Province of South Africa. The Tswana, the main group in present-day Botswana, were part of this great migration.

As time went on, the large group of people began to break up. Sometimes people moved away because frequent droughts made it difficult for large groups to find enough water. Also, as clashes occurred within chiefdoms, a group might leave to form its own community. These communities formed new clans related by language and culture. By the early 1700s some of these people had moved into the area we know today as Botswana.

The Tswana faced hostilities from outside their own community as well. Throughout the region to the south, people including the Tswana were fleeing in mass migrations. They were trying to get away from Shaka, the fierce Zulu leader. Shaka's well-trained and disciplined armies conquered vast territories. The people living in the region were not strong enough to fight back. When they were able to, the people fled, leaving their villages for safer areas. In the early 1800s many people were pushed off their lands. One group, the Ndebele, moved into the region where the Tswana lived. The Ndebele eventually made their way farther north, to the country now called Zimbabwe. The Tswana stayed around the Limpopo River valley where they established settlements. Here they found the best conditions for growing food and keeping livestock.

A William Burchell painting of a village

EARLY EXPLORERS

Europeans first settled in southern Africa in the 1600s after the Dutch arrived at the Cape of Good Hope. Over the next two hundred years, they began to make their way north into the interior.

Perhaps the first white man to travel in the region was William Burchell. He was a naturalist who traveled through the region in 1811 to study the wildlife and the terrain. While staying among the Tswana and San, Burchell worked on a Tswana dictionary. He drew careful maps of the region and illustrated his writings with paints made from local vegetable juices or animal blood. In his diaries he commented on everything he saw. Burchell was a keen observer. From his diaries we know that white hunters had already eliminated many wild animals from the Cape Colony, now part of South Africa. Burchell's zebra, a species found today throughout southern and eastern Africa, including Botswana, was named for him. His diaries and colored drawings were published in the 1820s and inspired many others to follow in his footsteps.

By the time Cornwallis Harris reached the region in 1836, he found evidence of the invasions by the Zulu people led by Shaka. Their brutal warfare pushed the Tswana out of the region south of the Limpopo River, into the more arid lands just to the north.

Like Burchell, Harris published accounts of his adventures and observations that provide much of our knowledge of the region at that time. Although the Tswana and the other African nations that lived in the region had full knowledge of their own history and were familiar with the natural world around them, they did not record their thoughts and observations in written accounts. But they did have oral histories. Many nations in Africa have storytellers, called *griots*, who know the whole history of their people. They tell the history over and over, and pass it along to each new generation. The written accounts we have were provided by explorers and missionaries. Each looked at the same information from his own point of view.

Many white men came to explore the region for personal reasons—often for the sense of adventure. For many, adventure meant killing as many animals as possible. They came very close to wiping out all the elephants in the Kalahari.

The other group of explorers was missionaries who came to convert the people to their form of religion.

By 1820 Robert Moffat of the London Missionary Society, a Protestant group, had settled in the region at Kuruman. Moffat was an unsuccessful missionary, but he started the first school for the Tswana (about 1815). His son-in-law, Dr. David Livingstone, was established in the region by 1843 and had his own mission

Robert Moffat (left) and Dr. David Livingstone (right)

station among the Bakwena, near present-day Molepolole. Livingstone lived in the region for ten years.

Dr. Livingstone became known for his explorations. He traveled around the edges of the Kalahari, searching for Lake Ngami, and eventually reached it in 1849. Although he is known as the first white man to see the lake, the credit should really go to the man who led his expedition, Cotton Oswell.

The missionaries played a complex role in the lives of the people. They helped the Tswana to keep control over their lands, and made it possible for some to learn to read and write. But they also brought guns into the region in an attempt to help the Tswana protect themselves.

ADVANCE OF THE BOERS

While Shaka was forcing people out of his area, pressure was also being exerted by the growing number of Europeans in the

A Boer farm in South Africa

area. The two main groups of white people—the British and the Dutch—who had settled in South Africa had completely different ways of living. The Dutch, mainly farmers known as Boers, kept moving into the interior in an effort to find farmland that was not ruled by the British. But there were few areas that were not already home to some people and, in time, the Boers intruded on the land of the Tswana. The Boers not only took over the lands but claimed all the people living there as their subjects. The Boers expected to use the Tswana as an unpaid labor force.

In response, the Tswana split into two main groups. One group moved back to part of the region now called the Transvaal. It would remain an important center for the Tswana from that time forward. It was clear that the Boers, with their superior weapons and endless desire for more land and people to work it, could not

A reenactment of the Boers fighting as they advanced through southern Africa

be stopped by the Tswana alone. The Tswana needed a powerful ally or protector.

The British ruled much of the land to the south. As early as 1867 the Tswana had asked the British for protection when gold was discovered in the Tati region, the best farmland along the Limpopo River. They knew that this discovery, along with the discovery of diamonds around the Vaal River in the Transvaal, would bring many more Europeans into the region as prospectors. At one point, the Boer-run government of the Transvaal announced that it was annexing much of the land around the Limpopo River. When the British protested the claim was dropped, but it was clear that such claims would continue to threaten the Tswana.

To protect themselves and their commercial interests, the British were finally pushed into protecting the Tswana. The Boers were continually pushing for more territory. In 1880 the Boers and British fought a war that ended in a British defeat. When the Boers kept pushing into the area north of the Molopo River, it finally became clear to the British that they would have to declare a protectorate in the region to ensure their own claims. The Tswana would finally get their protection, if only as a result of British self-interest.

BRITISH PROTECTORATES

The British set up a protectorate—that is, an area under their protection—around the Molopo River. The people didn't want to be a colony of Great Britain, which was the usual designation for territory claimed in Africa. Being a colony would put the land and its people under the rule of the British. The Tswana just wanted protection from the Boers. The protectorate was soon expanded to take in more territory, up to a point just north of the Chobe River. The protectorate was divided into two areas. The portion south of the Molopo River became known as British Bechuanaland and was considered a British colony. In 1889 it was incorporated into the Cape Colony and eventually became part of the Union of South Africa.

On September 30, 1885, the remainder of the territory, by far the larger part, became the Bechuanaland Protectorate. The dikgosi were divided about this change. Two of the principal dikgosi—Khama and Gaesitsiew—welcomed this protection of their lands and people. But another kgosi, Sebele, was opposed to the idea—and all the leaders feared losing their sovereignty. The

Cecil Rhodes,
the owner
of the British
South Africa Company

British were reluctant to be involved. They did not want to spend money defending or developing this region. They only wanted to protect the route to the north where their other territories were located.

CECIL RHODES

To get the most out of the territory while spending the least, Great Britain allowed it to be developed by private companies. This idea soon evolved into allowing a private company to virtually take over the territory. The company was the British South Africa Company (BSAC), owned by Cecil Rhodes. The BSAC was becoming a huge mining company. A railroad was crucial to Rhodes' dreams of creating a mining empire and making Great Britain the dominant power on the African continent. To do this, Rhodes wanted to build a railroad from the "Cape to Cairo"—from Cape Town at the southern tip of Africa to Cairo, Egypt, at the northern end. This was an ambitious plan for a time in which there were great tracts of land that were still virtually unexplored by Europeans. To build this railroad, strips of land had to be granted to Rhodes' company. Rhodes won his blocks of land, called the Lobatse, Gaborone, and Tuli blocks.

Between 1894 and 1897 Rhodes managed to build a good part of his railroad between Mafeking, the capital of the territory, and Bulawayo, in present-day Zimbabwe—a total of 400 miles (644 kilometers). The BSAC led by Rhodes was fighting to have Bechuanaland brought under its control. The British had promised the Tswana not to take away their self-rule. Now they were not only going back on that promise, they were turning the lives of the people over to an individual businessman by granting him a concession over the territory.

DIKGOSI FIGHT BACK

The three principal dikgosi—Khama, Sebele, and Bathoen— traveled to England in 1895 to meet with the British colonial secretary, Joseph Chamberlain. They knew that in Rhodesia (the territory to the north that was named for Rhodes and is now called Zimbabwe) the people had lost control over their land and every aspect of their lives. The dikgosi did not want to see their own lands and people become the property of Rhodes and his

*In 1895 the dikgosi (left) — Bathoen, Khama, and Sebele —
traveled to England to meet with Joseph Chamberlain
(right), the British colonial secretary.*

BSAC. Traveling to England was an extraordinary thing to do.
African chiefs, no matter how well educated, rarely left their own
villages. Traveling to England by boat took a month in each
direction. Chamberlain refused to help the dikgosi. However, the
dikgosi received the support of many church leaders in England
with the help of the London Missionary Society. Many other
British groups also supported the dikgosi. These groups believed
that the British government should be responsible for its own
territories and not turn them over to a commercial enterprise.

As a result, the three leaders were granted lands, called
"reserves," for their people. And the leaders granted a narrow
strip of land to be used for the railway. While they were making
these agreements, Rhodes and his agents back in Bechuanaland
were making deals with other dikgosi to secure as much land as
they could.

Chapter 3

LIFE UNDER THE BRITISII

COLONIAL RULE

In the Bechuanaland Protectorate, the British were faced with a colonial situation that was unique. The dikgosi were not all-powerful chiefs who imposed their will on others. They ruled with the cooperation of the people. The people lived in large villages, sometimes with as many as thirty thousand inhabitants. They gathered in the few places where water was available. A key feature of Tswana life was the *kgotla*, a meeting place where important matters were discussed. Among the Tswana people, every adult male could speak out, argue, and offer and receive advice. Free speech was recognized, encouraged, and made an integral part of the culture. Although the dikgosi could ignore the criticisms of their people, they were required to listen. The kgotla system became part of Tswana culture before the nineteenth century.

The dikgosi were educated men who faced the British with a knowledge of the law. When they felt that the British were putting unfair taxes on them, for example, they tried to use the British system of laws and justice to argue their case. They felt they had a better chance of protesting against colonial rule if they used the system set up by the colonizers.

In the beginning of the twentieth century, the hut tax was collected (left) and receipts were stamped (right).

THE BURDEN OF TAXES

Although some like to think of the British as the "best" of the colonial rulers, they followed many of the same practices in Bechuanaland as did other Europeans who ruled other African territories. The British used the dikgosi to carry out their decisions and to collect the taxes they imposed. The British set a tax on the people to pay the costs of administering the Bechuanaland Protectorate. These taxes weighed most heavily on the poorest people.

The first of these was the Hut Tax, a tremendous burden on the local people, who until that time had no need to be in a cash economy. They had been able to sustain themselves entirely by raising their own food, making their own clothes, and building their own huts. This was followed by the Native Tax, calculated in addition to the Hut Tax.

THE NEED FOR JOBS

To pay these taxes, the people had only two choices. Those who owned cattle could sell some to meet the new obligation. Those who had no cattle, however, had to seek employment. In Bechuanaland, there was virtually no wage-paying employment available. So although the Tswana originally had asked the British for protection to avoid being taken over by the British South Africa Company, the people now were forced to go to the Transvaal, part of South Africa, to find work. Both men and women became part of the migrant labor pattern, spending large periods of time—as much as a year or more—in and around Johannesburg before returning home to see their families. Some of them went to work in the mines, but many more worked as laborers in a variety of industries. Many of the women became maids in white households. The more educated men became clerks. Many worked for the railroads.

For the Tswana, these new taxes coincided with the loss of their cattle, their major source of wealth. In 1895 a disease called *rinderpest* struck the nation's cattle. This devastating disease moves rapidly through a herd when any of the animals is infected. It is thought to have killed more than 90 percent of the cattle in the protectorate. Although the herd was restored over the next decades, at the moment when people most needed cattle to pay their taxes they were left with almost none.

THE RESERVES

The loss of cattle was not the only problem. The vast territory of Bechuanaland offered little in the way of farmland or grazing for the cattle. When all of the people were able to make use of all of the land, allowing their cattle to graze wherever there was forage and letting the land rest in between, the problem of living in such an arid climate was less difficult. But by 1899 the land had been divided up into reserves. Each clan was confined to its own reserve. This restricted the people's movement and their ability to make use of marginal lands during times of scarcer rainfall.

Much of the best farmland had been turned over in "blocks" to white farmers or reserved for the British government. Some of these blocks had been signed away as concessions by various leaders as far back as the middle 1850s. Khama III, one of the three dikgosi who traveled to England to protest against Rhodes, gave the Tuli block, along the railroad near the South Africa border and one of the few fertile areas of the territory, to the British in 1895. This land eventually was sold to white farmers. Africans who lived in Francistown and Lobatse, the major towns in the area, were forced to live in segregated black townships.

RACIAL INEQUALITY

The way people were treated in Bechuanaland, as in all the other colonies in Africa, was determined by their race. Although blacks made up nearly all the population of the protectorate, they could only ride as third and fourth-class passengers on trains. Separate schools were set up, with little money spent on the few schools for blacks. Even in these, geography and history focused on European and white South African subject matter, not on the history or culture of the students or the geography of the area where they lived. Until 1932 no school above the primary level existed for blacks in the protectorate. A small number of privileged Batswana traveled to South Africa or England for higher education.

But the Bechuanaland Protectorate had a number of well-educated dikgosi who played significant roles in improving the lives of the people they ruled. They continued the system of ruling with the consent of the people, helping them adjust to the changes brought by the British. The kgotla system maintained by the dikgosi laid the foundation for the emerging democracy at indepedence.

EARLY LEADERS

Each of the eight major Tswana clans was ruled by its own kgosi, who made decisions affecting every phase of life. One of the most successful of these leaders during the early part of the twentieth century was Seepapitso II. During his leadership, from 1910 to 1916, he created a written record of his rule. He saw to the construction of schools, dams, and roads, and made sure that the Hut Tax was used to improve local living conditions. Like many of the leaders of the period, he spoke English.

Isang Pilane led the people from 1921 to 1929. In 1923 he directed the building of Mochudi National School, the largest building in the protectorate at that time. He also helped his people to learn modern agricultural skills.

At about the same time, from 1918 to 1939, Sebele II ruled the Bakwena. Sebele II was a more traditional ruler who permitted such practices as male initiation ceremonies and polygamy. He had spent time as a clerk in South Africa's mines, and also had

The Mochudi National School (left) was begun by Isang Pilane (right) to educate the people and to teach modern agricultural skills.

served in the South African army on the battlefields of Europe. He saw what the future of his people would be if South Africa were able to establish its racist rule in Bechuanaland.

RESIDENT COMMISSIONERS

Although the dikgosi were responsible for the direct, day-to-day rule of their people, the British government appointed resident commissioners to oversee the territory. The commissioners were actually in command of the affairs of the protectorate. In 1930 Charles Rey was installed as resident commissioner. He immediately made changes in the protectorate. He was determined to be rid of Sebele, whose ability to balance traditional and modern life and his influence over the other dikgosi threatened British control. Sebele was forcibly removed from office and sent to jail in a remote corner of Bechuanaland without a trial.

Tshekedi Khama fought against incorporating Bechuanaland into South Africa.

But the people wanted Sebele back and decided to appeal to the British sense of fair play. They drew up a petition that asked for Sebele's return or else a proper trial. It was signed by representatives of almost every Bakwena family. The British responded by ignoring the petition and insisting the Bakwena move to a new location in the town of Molepolole. The Bakwena refused until the next resident commissioner, Charles Arden-Clarke, arrived. He had their homes destroyed, fined them, and filled the jails with those who couldn't pay the fine. Sebele was never released from jail. He spent the last eight years of his life as a political prisoner.

RULING THE BANGWATO

In 1925 Tshekedi Khama became the acting head of the Bangwato. He stood in for the next kgosi, Seretse Khama, who was then only four years old. Seretse was Tshekedi's nephew and the son of Sekgoma II, who had ruled the Bangwato until his death. Tshekedi Khama was to act on his nephew's behalf until Seretse was old enough to assume his title. Tshekedi Khama came to play a major role in the affairs of the protectorate almost up to the time of independence.

Tshekedi Khama was a strong champion of rights for his people, and ultimately for all the people of the territory. He fought hard against granting mining concessions to the British South Africa Company. He had seen the way miners were treated in South Africa. Tshekedi Khama thought it would be better for the people to learn more about agriculture and dairy farming.

FIGHTING INDIRECT RULE

Tshekedi's fight against mining concessions came at the same time that another, even more difficult, situation presented itself. Charles Rey, the resident commissioner, wanted to do away with the whole system of the dikgosi. Rey felt that the dikgosi were standing in the way of progress and development. The plan Rey proposed was similar to the system of "indirect rule" used by the British in their other African colonies. Traditional leaders were to be used to carry out colonial administration. But when the proclamation was presented to the dikgosi in 1932, it was clear that traditional institutions such as the kgotla and democratic discussion of the community's needs would be destroyed if the plan were adopted. Tshekedi realized that this plan was like the system that was in place in South Africa. The African leaders there had been turned into clerks whose positions and power were totally controlled by the whites.

Tshekedi led the other dikgosi in protesting against the plan. One of his great fears, which had never been put to rest, was that at some point the British would hand Bechuanaland over to South Africa to govern. The version of indirect rule that was presented seemed to indicate this was a realistic fear. One of the most disturbing parts of the plan was the creation of councils that did not exist in traditional Tswana society. Although the Native Proclamations of 1934, which greatly reduced the independence of the people and replaced the dikgosi with British-appointed overseers, did become law, Tshekedi refused to comply with them and stalled until 1937, when there was a change in resident commissioners. In 1943, new proclamations were issued that were far more acceptable to the people.

FIGHTING BRITAIN'S WARS

As soon as Bechuanaland came under British control, it began to play a role in the various wars Britain fought. As early as the Boer War of 1899 to 1902, many Tswana served alongside the British as laborers, scouts, and even as soldiers. During World War I Tswana fought and worked on the British side in South West Africa (Namibia) as well as in Europe.

In 1939 when World War II erupted, some of the dikgosi, led by Tshekedi, were anxious for the protectorate to take part in the war. They hoped that this would prove to be a kind of insurance, to protect them against incorporation into South Africa. But when the British accepted the offer, the dikgosi found that their men did not want to go to war. The dikgosi forced them to go by preventing the men from working in the mines, denying them a way to earn a living. Ultimately, more than ten thousand men played a role in the war as part of the African Auxiliary Pioneer Corps. They served behind the lines and some fought against the

Germans in North Africa. The people left behind had trouble growing enough food to feed themselves as well as trying to grow extra food for the soldiers. It was Bechuanaland's real introduction into the Western world.

Before the war an economy had been established that made the people of Bechuanaland dependent on South Africa for work. During the frequent droughts in the region, people could earn money to buy food by working outside the territory. With so many adult men and women working outside the country, there was a growing division between the people living in the rural areas and those who were learning city ways. Many of those who stayed behind were wealthier people who were able to live off their cattle.

FIGHTING SOUTH AFRICAN RULE

The constant fear that South Africa would take over the Bechuanaland Protectorate grew even stronger in 1947, when South Africa appealed to the new United Nations to incorporate South West Africa into the Union of South Africa as its fifth province. Tshekedi feared that if this were allowed to happen, Bechuanaland would be next. The two territories shared a long border, and many refugees from South West Africa had fled into Bechuanaland. They were living proof of what the future could bring if South Africa were allowed to take over. Ultimately South Africa's request was denied, but the threat of South African rule remained real for the Tswana. This threat became even more troublesome in 1948 when the policy of *apartheid*, the separation of the races, was instituted in South Africa.

Seretse Khama and his wife, Ruth

SERETSE KHAMA

Tshekedi Khama had been standing in for his nephew Seretse as chief of the Bangwato since 1925. During those years, the young man had grown up, been educated in England, and become a lawyer. It was time for him to come home to Bechuanaland and assume his place as kgosi. But there was a major stumbling block. In 1948, just before he was to return, he married a white Englishwoman named Ruth Williams. To Tshekedi and to many others at the time, this created a scandal. Tshekedi did not believe the Bangwato would accept a white woman as their kgosi's wife. But when Seretse came back to Bechuanaland, his intelligence, personality, and political skills made a tremendous impression on the people, and they supported his marriage and his installation as chief.

But the Bangwato did not have the final say in the matter. The British at that time were still trying to maintain good relations with South Africa. They found themselves under great pressure not to accept Seretse Khama because his marriage to a white woman challenged colonial ideas about racial segregation. Because the British could not find any legal way to deny Seretse his position, they resorted to the illegal. He was brought to London on the pretense of discussing the future, then banned from his office and not allowed to return home. Tshekedi also was exiled in 1950. The British installed their own choice for kgosi, Rasebolai Kgamanee. But the Bangwato would not accept Kgamanee and conflicts emerged.

For six years the British kept Seretse out of Bechuanaland, except for brief visits. But Britain's efforts to please the South Africans were useless. The two countries drew far apart after the Nationalist government in South Africa put its apartheid policies into effect. In 1956 Seretse finally was permitted to return home, but only if he promised not to occupy the seat of power. This crisis proved to be a turning point for Bechuanaland. It helped many people begin to see themselves as part of a nation. For instance Tshekedi lived among the Bakwena during his exile— forging his sense of a unified nation. Further, they saw that only if the different regions united were they going to free themselves of British rule.

ROAD TO INDEPENDENCE

At the same time that Seretse Khama was fighting to take his rightful place in Bechuanaland, other leaders were emerging. A growing body of well-educated men wanted to take a role in the development of their homeland. The only place where they could exercise their leadership abilities was in a council set up by the British in 1920. Originally called the Native Advisory Council, it was renamed the African Advisory Council in 1940. Established under pressure from the dikgosi, the council had no real power, but it gave Africans a place to get together, to share views, and to approach the British with the strength of a common voice in important matters such as opposing incorporation into South Africa. Through the years the members had been asking the British government to create a legislative council, a step toward self-government. The resident commissioner, supported by white farmers, shop owners, and others, strenuously resisted such demands.

This was a delicate moment in the development of the protectorate. If such a legislative council were formed, it would bring in leaders who had not achieved their positions through the traditional, hereditary path of the dikgosi. During this period, tribal councils were established in the reserves, and these proved to be an important element in the transition to self-government.

By 1950 a joint advisory council had been established and its members, including both Tshekedi Khama and Seretse Khama, worked on establishing a legislative council. Tshekedi died in 1959, but the advisory council was successful.

On December 21, 1960, the Bechuanaland Protectorate Legislative Council became a reality. Although its members had struggled long and hard for this moment, the council gave Africans little authority. Africans represented 98 percent of the population, but they were only allocated one-third of the votes so the whites could keep control. Still, it was an important step on the road to independence because by permitting this body to exist, the British had committed themselves to giving up control. One of the most important functions the council fulfilled was getting people from different communities to discuss their needs and interests openly.

PREPARING FOR SELF-GOVERNMENT

By 1963 the British government was preparing to declare the independent government of Botswana, as the new country would be called. A Legislative Assembly was created to replace the council. All adults were going to be eligible to vote. The dikgosi would still be represented in their own "House of Chiefs," although this body would have no real power.

The dikgosi were quickly being replaced by politicians who were forming their own centers of power—political parties. The parties were meant to appeal to many more people than those living under the dikgosi. Among the most successful was the Bechuanaland Democratic party (BDP), led by Seretse Khama. Though Seretse never took his place as kgosi, he was the real leader of the Bangwato people and had strong ties throughout the protectorate. The BDP established a newspaper, edited by Quett

Before he became president, Quett Masire edited a newspaper to publicize the Bechuanaland Democratic party.

Masire, to publicize their organization. Masire traveled widely to address district meetings and became known to many people.

Although there were a number of political parties by the time the elections were held in 1965, the well-organized BDP won an overwhelming victory. It received 80 percent of the total vote. The elections were noteworthy because they were peaceful, although several political parties participated. The country had successfully made the transition from a territory of dikgosi to a modern nation ruled by the choice of the majority. On September 30, 1966, Botswana gained independence.

Seretse Khama opened Parliament (above) when Botswana became independent.
Princess Marina, a cousin of Queen Elizabeth of Great Britain,
represented Britain. A rally was held before free
elections (below). Tsholetsa, probably a campaign slogan, means "to lift up."

Chapter 4

FREEDOM COMES TO BOTSWANA

STARTING OVER

When Botswana became an independent country it had virtually no known natural resources, a harsh climate, and almost no facilities such as roads, schools, and health clinics left over from its days as a British protectorate. Botswana didn't even have its own capital. It had been administered from Mafeking in South Africa. In 1965, just before independence, the British erected buildings to house the new government in Gaborone, a small town close to the border with South Africa. The nation of Botswana began life with a crisis: a five-year-long drought that began just before independence. About one-third of all the cattle in the country died for lack of grazing and water. Crops failed, too, as the rain remained well below average year after year. The new government had to set up famine relief programs, especially for those people who had lost or sold their cattle and had no money to buy food.

ECONOMY RECOVERS

With support from Britain, Botswana made its way through those first years. By 1969, thanks to better rainfall than usual,

Farmers learn how to use a plow at an agricultural school

many farmers were able to resume growing food. Grazing improved and the nation's herds began to recover. The new government had much to do to fulfill its plans for modernization. When the British left, the country had only five miles (eight kilometers) of paved roads. There were scarcely any schools or hospitals. Few areas had electricity or clean water. The country did have a good network of veterinary services for the cattle herds, but otherwise it was a country that needed virtually everything and had little in the way of financial resources to begin building a modern nation.

NATIONAL GOALS

The government of Botswana, headed by President Seretse Khama from 1966 until his death in 1980, set itself four national goals: democracy, development, self-reliance, and unity. These goals were to be achieved through social justice, rapid economic growth, economic independence, and sustained development. One of the most effective tools Botswana had to reach these goals was a uniquely open and free society where government officials acknowledged the country's problems along with its successes.

SUDDEN WEALTH

In 1966 when Botswana became independent, it had one of the least promising economic outlooks of any emerging African country. That changed dramatically with the discovery of diamonds in 1967. Although it took four years before mining could start, the promise of considerable wealth gave the fledgling government a remarkable advantage in planning for the future. The intelligent use of resources to create the badly needed schools, roads, water systems, and electric power stands out as a testament to Botswana's leaders. Seretse Khama and his successor, Quett Masire, put Botswana's newfound wealth to work for all the people.

DIAMOND MINING

Botswana's diamond wealth was undiscovered at the time of independence. Geologists had been trying to discover the source of three diamonds they had found in a riverbed in 1956. In 1967, they made the first of three major finds in Botswana. This was the enormous diamond pipe at Orapa, on the edge of the Kalahari Desert. Diamond pipes are huge funnel shapes of volcanic origin that may lie just below the surface of the earth and extend deep into it. The pipe at Orapa measures 1 mile (1.6 kilometers) across at the surface and is one of the biggest diamond finds in the

A terraced pit at the Orapa diamond mine

world. When the mine was opened by President Seretse Khama, he said, "The wealth from Orapa is the key to Botswana's development."

The diamonds were found by geologists from De Beers, the huge South African mining firm that is involved in diamond mining operations all over southern Africa. De Beers was particularly excited about the discovery of diamonds in Botswana because the new mines offered a fresh and important source for diamonds. Finding a profitable new diamond pipe is a very expensive undertaking. Only one out of a hundred pipes found contains enough diamonds to be worth mining. The Botswana mines are operated on a 50-50 partnership basis between De Beers and the Botswana government. The company is called Debswana Diamonds. Thanks to taxes as well as its share of profits, Botswana receives more than 70 percent of its foreign exchange income from the mines.

Although prospecting had been undertaken in Botswana for many years, the diamonds were found just after independence. This made it easier for the new Botswana government to make a very good financial deal with De Beers. Botswana shared in the investment in building the mines, but relied on De Beers' expertise. Botswana earns about one billion dollars a year from its diamond industry, the basis of its economy. These mines are expected to produce substantial quantities of diamonds for at least another fifty years.

Botswana is the largest producer of gem diamonds in the world. But a large part of the total production is industrial diamonds, used in many manufacturing processes. Diamonds are the hardest substance known, and can be used to keep machine parts from rubbing against each other. Industrial diamonds are used to cut through marble, polish parts of automobiles, and make grooves in concrete runways. There are thousands of uses for industrial diamonds.

CREATING THE MINES

Most diamond mines start at the rock face and are worked as open pits until the mine gets deep. The pipe at Orapa and the two other mines operated in Botswana, Letlhakane and Jwaneng, are huge. They will be worked as open pits for many years. Yet they were almost missed. The only indication of a diamond mine is a scattering of certain minerals at or near the surface of the mine.

At Jwaneng, the mouth of the pipe starts 150 feet (46 meters) beneath the Kalahari sands. It was only found after samples of the rock were brought to the surface. Jwaneng was a much bigger technological challenge and a much more expensive mine to

At Jwaneng diamond mine, much digging had to be done to reach the pipe (above). An employee swimming pool at Orapa diamond mine (above right)

create than Orapa. At each mine in Botswana an entire town had to be built by De Beers to accommodate the employees, providing housing and all other services such as schools, medical facilities, and places for sports and recreation for the miners and their families. Water is piped in from sources 30 to 40 miles (48 to 64 kilometers) away. But the expense is well worth it. The geologists estimated that Jwaneng would produce at least six million carats a year and their expectations already have been exceeded.

TRAINING NEW WORKERS

Debswana has built training schools for its employees. In addition to the employment at the mine itself, the Botswana government has encouraged Debswana and others to build diamond-cutting facilities in the country. These offer training, employment, and additional income for the workers and the

At Teemane Manufacturing Company, a worker checks a cut diamond (left). Many of the employees at Teemane are young Batswana women (right).

nation. A diamond cutting and polishing factory called Teemane Manufacturing Company was opened in Serowe in November 1992. It employs five hundred people, many of them young Batswana women.

THE MINING PROCESS

Twice a week, a section of the mine is blasted loose. After the dust settles, working with huge mechanical shovels, the crews of men collect all the rocks. After the ore is picked up, it is brought to a treatment plant. The rock must be crushed and pulverized before the diamonds can be separated from the surrounding gravel.

Jwaneng, the newest mine, began operations in 1982. It took two years to remove the top layers of desert sand before the actual

*A blasting line is put into the rock (left) and
a section is blasted loose (right).*

mining could begin. By 1991 the total production from Jwaneng
alone reached more than nine million carats, equal to more than
half the total of the three mines. About one-third of Jwaneng's
production is of gem-quality diamonds. The rest are used in
industry.

All of this production is not entirely good news, however.
When the world's economy slowed down in the 1980s and early
1990s, the demand for diamonds also slowed. Because of weak
demand, Botswana had to stockpile about 10 percent of its yearly
production from 1982 to 1985. In 1987 De Beers purchased
Debswana's stockpile, which was then estimated to have a value
of more than $500 million. At the same time, the government
received a 5.2 percent share in De Beers Consolidated Mines of
South Africa. It also now has two members on De Beers' board of
directors, an indication of just how important Botswana's
diamonds are to De Beers.

Headquarters of Debswana in Gaborone

FRAGILE ECONOMY

The dependence on diamonds for such a large part of Botswana's economy is troubling. As other countries in Africa have learned, a one-crop or one-mineral economy is fragile. The slightest change in the world market for that product can mean a dramatic drop in income.

The Central Selling Organization (CSO), the marketing arm of De Beers, controls prices by making sure that at least 85 percent of the diamonds mined each year become part of its stock. In the 1990s the stockpile grew larger and larger. There were two reasons for this growing pile of unsold diamonds. First, the worldwide recession meant a decrease in sales of diamonds to consumers. Secondly, the problem was made more severe because of the enormous number of gem diamonds being mined in Botswana. In 1991 the CSO told suppliers like Debswana to keep 25 percent of the diamonds in their own stockpile. It promised to buy them in the future but in the meantime, Debswana had to wait for the income. That meant the Botswana government had 25 percent less revenue.

Diamond revenue has financed most of the investment in education, health care, and village water systems that bring water

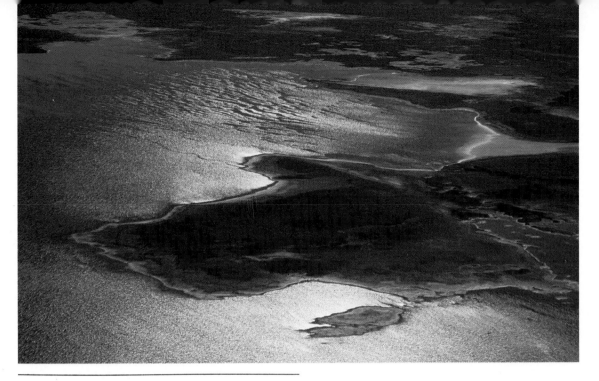

An aerial view of the Makgadikgadi Pan

to rural households. Any decrease in this income means the government will have to slow down its goals for better education, health care, and other important social welfare programs.

Nearly all the rough diamonds mined in the world are bought and marketed by the CSO. Although the CSO is based in London, it is tied to its parent company in South Africa. After fighting so hard to remain free of South Africa during all the years leading up to independence, Botswana now finds itself closely tied to this South African company. Still, Botswana is much better off having the diamond income than it would be without it.

OTHER MINERALS

Diamonds are not the only mineral found in Botswana. Far less valuable but still contributing to the economy is the soda ash plant at Sua Pan. (*Sua* means "salt" in one of the San languages. A pan is a natural depression or basin in the land.) Located at the

Workers drill holes for placing dynamite at the Morupule coal mine.

edge of the vast Makgadikgadi Pan, this plant processes soda ash and salt that occur naturally in this vast, flat plain. The plant provides employment and training opportunities for the local people in an area that had few opportunities for paid labor. Soda ash is used in the manufacture of many products for industry and for household use. The salt produced is also used domestically (for flavoring food) and in industry.

Botswana also mines other minerals, notably copper, nickel, and a small amount of gold. The gold is mined principally around Francistown, an area where there was a considerable gold rush in the 1890s. Copper, mined in ancient times, and nickel are both found and worked at Selebi-Phikwe. The two metals occur together and must be separated and refined before they can be sold. This process is performed at the Selebi-Phikwe smelter.

The different minerals make different contributions to the economy. Copper is found in many places in Africa and sells for $1 a pound. Diamonds sell for a few dollars a carat in the case of an industrial diamond to thousands of dollars a carat for a fine gem diamond. The size of an average engagement ring diamond is about one-quarter of a carat.

CATTLE

Before diamonds were found, beef was Botswana's most important export. Even in the colonial period, the attention paid to the health of cattle was significant. A veterinary department was set up in 1905. By fencing off areas where livestock diseases occurred, the government was able to control, and eventually eliminate, the most serious disease affecting cattle—hoof and mouth disease. This made it possible for Botswana's meat to pass the high standards of the European countries that are now the biggest importers.

In spite of periodic droughts, which often cause the death of one-third of the nation's herds, cattle are the most important agricultural product and one that provides income for the greatest number of people. Cattle are often kept at cattle posts out in the open, where they can graze. The big herds must be driven many miles from the grazing area to water, and often go two or three days without drinking. When the herds are small, they may be kept closer to home. The cattle owners build a hut for themselves and then build separate *kraals*, or "corrals," for the cattle, for the calves, and for the goats and sheep and other livestock.

By 1954 the first *abattoir*, or slaughterhouse, where cattle were killed and prepared for export, had been built at Lobatse. Before that time, nearly all sales were to South Africa. Once the slaughterhouse was built, the sales began to shift to Europe. In addition to the abattoir in Lobatse, the largest in Africa, the Botswana Meat Commission has built two additional slaughterhouses in Francistown and Maun, which together can handle 300,000 head of cattle a year. Today 95 percent of the beef is exported.

When conditions are good, the national herd numbers about three million head of cattle. For most of the people, especially in the rural areas, livestock (including goats and sheep) is important to their subsistence. But most cattle are raised with no intention of selling them for meat. For the Batswana, as for many of the people in Africa, cattle are considered wealth and a source of status. Even when conditions are poor, or bad, as they often are in such a climate, people are reluctant to sell their cattle for slaughter. It can mean a total change in their way of life, especially if they are not able to build up a herd again. Most families have additional sources of cash income, such as selling some of the food they grow or making household goods for others.

Traditionally those who kept cattle often held them at cattle posts that could be as much as 100 miles (161 kilometers) away from their homes. These areas offered water sources as well as grazing. The large herds resulted in overgrazing of pasturelands. In an effort to reduce the loss of Botswana's precious grazing areas, the government introduced the Tribal Grazing Land Policy (TGLP). This divided the land into three areas: communal lands for traditional grazing, commercial lands for large-scale ranching, and open areas to be held in reserve primarily for wildlife. Since TGLP was established, the differences between those who keep cattle as wealth and those who raise cattle for sale have increased, creating new differences between rich and poor. Conditions for keeping cattle as wealth are deteriorating. Owners have to find not only grazing for their cattle but also water. Often, cattle owners must dig holes in the ground, called boreholes, to reach water and bring it to the surface. Most cattle herds held as wealth are found in Botswana's central district.

Commercial ranchers, who raise cattle with the intention of

Cattle and people at a borehole

sending them to slaughter, see the cattle as a way of making money, not as money itself. This group of ranchers is small, only a few hundred, but they own tens of thousands more cattle than small-scale farmers. The beef-exporting business is in the hands of a few people, and it is primarily those people who benefit directly from the sale of the cattle.

CATTLE TREK

When they are fully grown and ready for slaughter the cattle must be transported, usually by railway, if they are coming from the eastern part of the country. But first they must reach the railroad and this often means trekking them through the bush to market. All across the open countryside, herds are moved along, driven by ranch hands, in a scene that resembles the Wild West image of America, with dust, heat, and the lowing of the cattle.

Loading water containers onto a donkey

Because the trip is so long, the ranch hands and the herd must spend many nights in the open. To protect the cattle from wild animals, the men build kraals of tree branches and drive the animals inside. They have to follow a route that takes them past boreholes where the cattle can be watered at least every few days. The cattle lose weight on the trek and that means a loss of income for the farmers. The best drivers are those who know how long to let the animals rest and browse along the way.

OTHER LIVESTOCK

In addition to cattle, most farming households raise sheep and goats for their own consumption. In fact, many households don't have cattle but do raise small stock. The investment in goats and sheep is smaller, and these animals are less susceptible to drought and require much less food than do cattle. While small stock also represent wealth, most of these animals are raised for food. They're kept in small kraals near the home. Many families keep chickens for their eggs and to eat. They keep donkeys for transport.

Maize (left), one of the main crops, is made into meal and cooked as porridge (right).

FARMING

Most agricultural production in Botswana uses a system of dryland farming, which depends entirely on rainfall. Dryland farming works best with drought-resistant crops such as sorghum. During the dry season, the crop may actually stop growing. When rain comes, growth begins again. Because of the irregular rainfall in Botswana, dryland farming often fails, and then no crop is produced at all.

Normally, Botswana grows barely one-third of the food it needs. In a drought year, this can fall to a small fraction of even this amount. The staple crop is the grain sorghum. About three-fourths of all the arable land is planted with sorghum. The other main crops are maize (corn), millet (another grain), and beans.

In Botswana, the land requires oxen for plowing. Because it is so difficult to maintain large livestock during the frequent periods of drought, more people lose the use of their land. Some people give up trying to grow their own food. While the population has grown rapidly since independence, the amount of food produced has not kept up with this growth; indeed, it has decreased significantly. This inability to grow food has been partly responsible for a rapid movement of the population from the rural areas to the cities. More than 10 percent of the people live in Gaborone.

Because so little of Botswana's land is suitable for farming and because rainfall is normally scarce, the government must import most of the country's basic food requirements. During times of drought, the relief program covering food distribution to rural households puts a great strain on the budget.

IRRIGATION PROBLEMS

Irrigation has been tried in only a few areas, around the Chobe and Limpopo rivers, by commercial farmers. It is difficult to find sources of water for irrigation. One plan that would have diverted the waters of the Okavango River for irrigation was shelved after widespread opposition from many people concerned about the Okavango Delta's overall environment. The impact of such a diversion on the wildlife in the region as well as on the single most important water source in Botswana was impossible to predict. There was no way to test it and then return to the natural environment if the plan failed. This might adversely affect the tourist industry, another important source of income. The ongoing need to find reliable sources for water is closely related to Botswana's potential for economic growth.

Chapter 5

BUILDING A MODERN NATION

THE ECONOMY

Botswana is divided into sixteen districts: Chobe, Ngamiland, Ghanzi, Kgalagadi, Kweneng, Kgatleng, Southern, South East, North East, Francistown, Gaborone, Lobatse, North West, Orapa, Selebi-Phikwe, and Central. Virtually all of the nation's economic life (other than the mines and Ghanzi cattle ranches) lies within a narrow strip that runs from the South East through the Central District to the North East. This is where most of the rainfall occurs, where the railroad runs, and where the major towns are found. It is also where 80 percent of the population lives.

The importance of diamonds to Botswana's economy might lead one to think that diamond mining provides a great deal of employment for the Batswana. Actually, only about 5,000 people are employed in Botswana's diamond mines. More Batswana still travel to work in the mines in South Africa. In 1990, 17,500 people—10 percent of all salaried workers—were employed there. But there is a big difference in the kinds of jobs and the kinds of lives these different mine jobs provide. Miners who work in

Botswana live near the mine with their families, in modern, comfortable housing. They hold a variety of jobs according to their education and skills. And they work in their own country. Miners who work in the mines in South Africa must travel far from their homes and families. Although the laws of apartheid have been officially changed, conditions remain much the same. When they are not in the mines, the miners live in hostels, like big dormitories, for men only. Living conditions are very harsh in the hostels, and violence often erupts in the close living quarters between men of different ethnic groups and different political beliefs.

Of the 230,000 Batswana who hold jobs of any kind, one-third of them work for government agencies. This is a problem for such a small economy. Too many people depend directly on the government for their livelihood.

Botswana is still in the process of educating its population, so there are many unskilled workers who need jobs and many skilled jobs that must go to workers from outside the country. It will probably take some time before Botswana's education system catches up and produces enough people trained to take over these better-paying, highly skilled jobs.

CREATING A STRUCTURE

To address the need for skills, one-fifth of the national budget is used for education. But it is difficult for housing and schooling to keep pace with the growing population. Nearly half the population is under the age of fifteen. This puts a tremendous strain on the educational system and on the need to provide food.

The manufacturing sector of the economy produces only 4

Left: Half of Botswana's population is under the age of fifteen.
Right: Solar cells have been installed on the roof of the gate house
at Chobe National Park.

percent of the country's total earnings, but employs twice as many
people as mining. For this reason, the introduction of new
industries is strongly encouraged. Botswana needs many new
jobs, most of which must be created by new investors.

INDUSTRY

Even in the face of South Africa's overwhelming control of
Botswana's markets, a number of companies have opened plants
in Botswana to make products for the local market. Among these
are a shoe factory, a company that makes fences and door and
window frames, and a garment firm that produces jackets, T-
shirts, and women's shirts. Several firms make equipment
designed to use solar energy — appropriate for a climate that is
almost always sunny.

The Botswana government encourages people to come to the
country and become residents and even citizens if they agree to

open businesses there, especially if they can employ local labor. The need for heavy construction, road surfacing, homes, and office buildings has brought in firms from many countries. The demand for industrial areas that are supplied with electricity and transportation connections has grown faster than the government can fulfill, but it expects to catch up. At the same time, housing units have been built by the thousands to take care of the many new employees in the towns.

ELECTRICITY

Electricity is one of the basic requirements of any modern society. Each year the Botswana Power Corporation (BPC) connects about two thousand households to the country's electrical system. By 1992 close to thirty thousand households enjoyed electricity.

The BPC devised an innovative means of charging for electricity to meet the local culture. The people were not used to receiving bills after a utility was used. So BPC set up a system of meters operated by tokens. Customers buy a certain amount of electricity in advance. When they use up the amount they have paid for, they purchase more tokens.

TRANSPORTATION

When Botswana became independent, it had only about five miles (eight kilometers) of paved road. But it did have a well-established railroad running through its heavily populated eastern corridor. This was actually a continuation of the line dreamed of by Cecil Rhodes. The line was operated by Zimbabwe (later called

Ximbabwe) Railways until 1987, when the Botswana government took control and put its own trained personnel in place.

Until the 1970s this was the only rail line in Botswana. The growing need to transport the nation's mineral production has encouraged the development of three new spur lines, including a 103-mile (166-kilometer) line between Francistown and Sua Pan, where the soda ash project is located, and a line between Morupule, where coal is mined, and Selebi-Phikwe, where the coal is needed in smelting furnaces. Botswana has invested in new freight carriers, locomotives, and passenger cars to upgrade a system and tracks that are nearly one hundred years old.

While the railroad was built immediately after the Bechuanaland Protectorate was proclaimed and the country was crisscrossed with footpaths, the territory had little in the way of roads. Today, there are about 9,942 miles (16,000 kilometers) of paved or hard-packed roads and rough tracks, of which about 1,553 miles (2,500 kilometers) are tarred.

In cooperation with Namibia to the west, a road is being constructed from Gaborone across the Kalahari to Windhoek, the capital of Namibia. Ultimately this road will reach Namibia's Atlantic Ocean port of Walvis Bay. Construction of this 777-mile (1,250-kilometer) road, the Trans-Kalahari Highway, should be completed by 1994. This would give landlocked Botswana access to ocean transport to the west and enable the country to increase its trade with countries other than South Africa.

With the recent peace accords signed in Mozambique and the end of most hostilities in that country, the important connection to the Indian Ocean port of Beira has been reestablished. Rail lines from Botswana up to Zimbabwe and then across to Beira are well established.

An Air Botswana plane (left) and an announcer for Radio Botswana (right)

Improvement of the roads around the country, including a road from Francistown to Maun, the heart of Botswana's tourism, is making travel much faster. It is now possible for farmers to bring their crops to market and to deliver cattle to Francistown by truck. A major road runs along the same route as the railroad, connecting Lobatse in the south with Gaborone, the capital, and Francistown in the north.

Throughout much of the rest of the country, road traffic is light. Some of these roads are quite rough. Most are suitable only for four-wheel-drive vehicles. This travel can be undertaken only with sufficient food, water, and gasoline to complete the journey.

AIR TRAVEL

The national airline, Air Botswana, flies to the capital cities of twelve neighboring or nearby African countries, including Johannesburg, South Africa; Harare, Zimbabwe; Lusaka, Zambia; Luanda, Angola; Nairobi, Kenya; and Windhoek, Namibia. An international airport located at Gaborone receives flights from Europe as well as from other African nations. Smaller airports are located at key cities around the country. A military air base is located near Mogoditshane, not far from Gaborone.

COMMUNICATION

In 1966 the Botswana government began its own radio station, Radio Botswana. It broadcasts in both English and Setswana. There are no commercials on this station, but the government is considering a second station that would offer commercial service. Transmitters carry the broadcast signal to most of the country. With projected expansion, some broadcasts will soon reach throughout the country.

Although there is no Botswana television service, private television clubs allow subscribers to receive signals from the South African Broadcasting Corporation as well as from Bophuthatswana, the part of South Africa where more than two million Tswana live. All Tswana, wherever they live, speak the same language. BopTV, as it is called, is the best-known commercial television service in southern Africa. It is a privately owned system, not controlled by the government.

Botswana has one government newspaper, the *Daily News*, available free of charge. A number of privately printed weekly newspapers also are published.

Telephone service is available in the major urban areas and villages, though few households have phones. Until 1986 all international phone calls had to be routed through South Africa, giving that country control over this aspect of Botswana's daily life. A modern phone system, introduced in 1986, permits international direct dialing to countries around the world, although not to neighboring countries. Ironically, Botswana is an example of a country where colonial neglect is occasionally a benefit. Because it had virtually no telephone system before, it has been able to leap ahead with modern electronic equipment.

Above: The people of the country—Batswana—are generally from one of eight clans.
Below: Some of the daily chores in a village are pounding sorghum or maize to make flour (left) and gathering firewood (right).

Chapter 6

DAILY LIFE IN BOTSWANA

Most of the people live in the eastern part of the country where there is the most rainfall, the most fertile land, and the best chance of farming and raising cattle. Only one of these clans, the Batawana, lives apart, in the northwest areas known as Ngamiland.

The Tswana people are known for their large traditional villages and for their democratic ways. They have a remarkable ability to govern themselves in a practical way, trying to make the most of their natural resources without ruining the land, and taking care of one another.

VILLAGE LIFE

Daily life in the villages revolves around taking care of the livestock and growing and preparing food. Much of this work is done by women. They pound grain, usually sorghum or maize, in big wooden containers to make flour. The flour is made into a porridge. This is the basic food of most of the people. Cooking is done over an open fire, and the usual fuel is wood, which the women must collect from the bush outside the villages.

Rondavels in a village near Gaborone

Houses are made of clay, then covered with a mixture of mud and cow dung, which is hard when it dries. The roof, made of thatch, is supported by a circle of wooden poles. These traditional homes are usually round and are called *rondavels*, but some people build them in a rectangular shape. They are grouped together as part of a large village. All the members of a family live close together.

Villagers also have a second home in a place known simply as *masimo*, or "the lands." Because they spend as much as six months at the lands, they build similar houses for themselves as a family group next to their fields. This is where villagers, especially the women, traditionally spent most of their time tending their crops, especially in the days before the road system was improved. Fewer people travel to the lands now, because the droughts have driven many off their farmland.

Left: Putting on a thatch roof
Right: These second homes have been built next to maize fields.

Families with cattle have a third home—the cattle post, or *moraka*. The men of the family usually stay at the cattle post to tend the cattle. Depending on the wealth of the family, young boys or men may be hired to care for the family's animals.

TAKING GOOD CARE

The tradition of taking good care was established by the dikgosi and was carried into modern times by the first president, Sir Seretse Khama. Khama was made a knight of the British Empire for his leadership at the time he became president, so the title "sir" is used.

Sir Quett Masire took office on the death of Sir Seretse in 1980 and was elected in his own right in 1984. During this period Botswana suffered two of the worst drought years the country has ever known.

President Masire reviewing army troops

When other countries in Africa suffer drought, headlines tell about the large numbers of people who die, often from mismanagement of the food aid given to them. President Masire has worked hard to be sure that none of the Batswana die of famine. His great effort was recognized by a United States organization called the Hunger Project. In 1989 Masire and a community leader from another African nation shared the Hunger Project's annual leadership prize. According to the Hunger Project, "President Masire's drought relief program . . . ensured that adequate food supplies were distributed across the country. When some countries in Africa were suffering from massive famine, not a single person in Botswana died of starvation." President Masire also was knighted by the Queen of England for his leadership.

The San people are struggling to survive in today's world.

SAN

The San are the original inhabitants of the land, and have been living here for as long as fifty thousand years. San refers to a diverse group of people who share certain common traits including their body size and shape, their facial features, and the way they live. Before the arrival of any other people, the San lived by hunting wild game and gathering the plants and roots they found. They have a unique ability to make use of what little they find on the land and to survive in the harsh conditions of the Kalahari.

Many of the San are small in height, about 5 feet (1.5 meters), with skin color ranging from yellowish-tan to a deeper, honey color. Their hair grows in tufts called "peppercorns." Many have a tilt to their eyes that gives their faces an Oriental cast.

San gatherers carry water in ostrich eggs (left)
and put plant poison on arrows (above) for hunting.

San lived as hunter gatherers. They made use of all the plants
found growing in the Kalahari: nuts, fruits, wild melons, roots,
and leaves. They made water carriers from ostrich-egg shells the
size of small cantaloupes. The San hunted the wild game that
lived in the area. They made poisons from certain plants and
applied the poison to the tips of their arrows. Because the poisons
worked slowly, it might take days for a large animal to die.
During this time the hunter would track the animal, day and
night if necessary. San are skillful trackers. They are able to pick
out tracks of a particular animal mixed with others in the sand.
Perhaps one thousand to two thousand San still live in the
traditional way in the central Kalahari. The great drought of 1990
pushed the rest of them out of the Kalahari.

San always shared the meat from a successful hunt with the
other families in their area. This sharing was quite exact, and each
person received an appropriate amount depending on kinship.

San women gather edible roots (left) and a man carries a duiker he has snared (right).

This ensured the survival of all the people. The next successful hunt might be carried out by someone else and each family could expect a share. Not only the meat was used. The hide, teeth, and horns were used. Nothing was ever wasted, and the San never killed an animal they didn't intend to eat. Anthropologist John Marshall's film, *The Hunters*, depicts this way of life.

LOSING GROUND

The San were essentially nomadic people and lived throughout Southern Africa. As other Africans and, later, whites advanced on their territories the San were driven deeper and deeper into the Kalahari, until they finally reached regions that were unlivable for anyone else. Through the centuries they managed to survive the worst droughts through their knowledge of where to dig for water and where to find food in the desert.

Though explorers passed through the fringes of the Kalahari on

John Marshall speaks with some of the people he films.

occasion, no white people stayed there until the Marshall family went in the 1950s to learn about the !Kung way of life. The Marshalls are a family of American anthropologists, Laurence and Lorna Marshall and their children, John and Elizabeth. (The !Kung are one of the San group; the ! is used to indicate a clicking sound that is difficult to show in writing.) Much of what we know of !Kung life comes from the Marshalls' work. Elizabeth Marshall wrote a popular account, *The Harmless People*. The fiction writer, Laurens van der Post, captured the past and present of the San in his books, *The Lost World of the Kalahari* and *A Story Like the Wind*.

The San passed on their lore, their myths, and the most detailed history of their people by telling stories. They preserved the story of their people through generations by these oral histories. No detail of a hunt or any important event in their lives was forgotten. When food was plentiful the San ate and ate until their bodies filled up and their skin became smooth. When food was scarce, they used up the extra fat and their skin would hang in wrinkles.

This San found water stored in a tree (above).
Right: San relax and listen to a home-made fiddle.

A DYING CULTURE

Those of us who will never travel to the Kalahari can find out about the way the San live from films. John Marshall made many films documenting !Kung life both before and after they had intensive contact with Bantu and with whites. A very popular film, *The Gods Must Be Crazy*, made by Jamie Uys, a South African filmmaker, shows in a fanciful way many of the special qualities of this way of life. In this film something modern, in this case a Coca-Cola bottle, comes into their life and creates envy, a trait that has no place in San life. But the traditional way of life shown in the film is virtually unknown among the San today.

No one knows how many San are left, but the usual estimate is about thirty thousand to sixty thousand in the Kalahari and perhaps fifty thousand of that number within Botswana. The world of the San has largely disappeared because their territory has been taken over. Even in the largely unlivable spaces of the Kalahari, there is enough grass for grazing cattle. Boreholes have been dug for water, and the San have come into contact with Western ways of life. After thousands of years of relatively unchanging life, the San culture has been overwhelmed.

The San are a dilemma to the Botswana government. Though few in number, they are among the best-known people in Africa. Everyone wants to see them and to see their way of life. Yet their traditional ways are simply not suitable for the modern country that Botswana is becoming. Even the land meant for them, the Central Kalahari Game Reserve, has been overrun by ranchers who bring their cattle in to graze. The San have sometimes been severely punished by game wardens in the reserves because of their poaching. Although the San have lived in harmony with wildlife through the centuries, they have often been the object of people's scorn and are sometimes forced to work for farmers for a little food. For a long time, many San have worked on cattle ranches in western Botswana, in and around Ghanzi, often under the poorest living conditions. Virtually no San people live by hunting and gathering anymore.

Organizations that are trying to help the San adapt to modern life include the Nyae Nyae Development Foundation; the Ju/Wa Development Foundation in Namibia, started by John Marshall and Megan Biesele; and the Kalahari People's Fund, started by anthropologist Richard Lee. These organizations help the people with their farming efforts. The San long ago saw the need to grow some of their own food, in addition to hunting and gathering.

Herero women wear long, brightly colored dresses with many petticoats and wrap their heads in turbans.

THE HERERO

A community of about twenty-five thousand Herero lives in the northwest part of the country. They are descended from those who fled Namibia in 1904 when they were being hunted down and killed by Germans. The Herero women dress in a distinctive style, wearing long, brightly colored dresses and many petticoats and wrapping their heads in matching turbans. They created this style because the missionaries insisted they cover their bodies. It was the Herero interpretation of the Victorian dress worn by the missionary wives.

*Lucas Mangope,
president of
Bophuthatswana*

WHITES IN BOTSWANA

From a handful of whites in Botswana at independence, there are now about fifteen thousand (1 percent of the population), many of them in Gaborone and wherever industrial complexes are found. Most of the large, commercial cattle ranches are owned and operated by white farmers.

BOPHUTHATSWANA

Although Botswana is the country of the Tswana people, more ethnic Tswana live in South Africa than in Botswana. These people, numbering about two million, are part of the Barolong group of Tswana. They live in the region of South Africa called Bophuthatswana. The city of Mafeking, which functioned as the capital of Bechuanaland until Botswana's independence, is an important city in Bophuthatswana. Bophuthatswana was declared "independent" by South Africa, and given its own president, Lucas Mangope, but no other country has ever recognized it as

*Some of the tourist attractions at Sun City are the
Bridge of Time (left) and the Valley of Waves (right).*

independent. It would be an unusual country, since it is not a real
territory. It is made up of bits of land scattered around South
Africa, many miles apart. Still, when South Africa decided
Bophuthatswana was independent in 1977, there was a big ceremony,
with marching bands and traditional Tswana dancing. The people
are real, it's just the political entity that has been made up.

Bophuthatswana is important to Botswana because many
Batswana go there to work and have relatives living there. There
is a great deal of traveling back and forth. Parts of
Bophuthatswana lie right next to Botswana's southern border.
Some Batswana even go there to shop. Many Batswana work in
the entertainment complex known as Sun City, which opened in
1980. In December 1992, the Miss World competition was held in
Sun City. One-and-a-half million visitors go there each year to
enjoy the complex of hotels and theaters, the exciting, open

atmosphere, and the gambling casinos. Gambling is not allowed in South Africa. By creating Sun City, South Africa found a way to allow gambling and yet not offend the many strictly religious people who live in South Africa and believe that gambling is a sin. It was also a place where people of different races could associate freely.

Before South Africa began to dismantle its policy of apartheid, entertainers from around the world refused to travel there to perform. Sun City was built to get around that. But most of the world's entertainers boycotted Sun City because they understood it was still part of South Africa.

EDUCATION

At the time of independence in 1966, fewer than one-fourth of Batswana children attended school. The schools built by the British were meant for the children of white colonial administrators and farmers. In other colonies and territories where the colonial powers did not provide schools and teachers mission schools filled this need. In Bechuanaland there were few such missions to play this role.

The Batswana taught traditional knowledge in a system of *mephato,* or "regiments," where children of the same age group were instructed in their cultural heritage. In some cases, the Batswana created their own Western education. Isang Pilane, who directed his people in the building of a huge school in 1923, was the first. He wanted the people to learn English, mathematics, and other skills so that they could remain at home rather than go to South Africa for paid work. Slowly schools were started in other villages as well. Not many Batswana were able to gain such skills

In the Kalahari Desert children play a game of soccer during their school lunch break

before independence. Those few wealthy Batswana parents who could afford to do so sent their children out of the country for their education.

At the time of independence there were 250 primary schools attended by about 75,000 children. But the population of the country was more than a half million, and at least half were young people. Many schools were simply places where classes could be held, often outdoors under trees or in temporary shelters. There were only 8 secondary schools, all of them private or run by missions. Any Batswana who made it past this level and wanted to go on to a university had to do so outside the country. In 1966 there were 50 such students.

A country that is not educating its own people has little chance to make informed decisions. The village meeting system had worked well for discussing problems in the past, but contemporary issues, political changes in the nations around them, and other late-twentieth-century concerns made it vital for the Batswana to have access to modern education.

Students taking examinations (left) and college students checking exam results at the University of Botswana (right)

After independence, the Botswana government made education one of its top priorities. Much of the money earned in the mining industries was funneled into education. Before there could be children in school, there had to be teachers, so the government established teachers' training colleges. There are now thirteen thousand teachers in training, preparing to educate the next generation of children.

By 1991 there were 640 primary schools, more than 9,000 teachers, and 275,000 primary-level students. For the first four years of school, children are taught in Setswana; then English is used. But there is a sharp decline in attendance after primary school. Only 50,000 children were in secondary schools, one-fifth of the number in the lower grades. This was not entirely because of a lack of interest. There were only 170 secondary schools in the country, too few to take all the students who wanted to continue.

The University of Botswana has an enrollment of about thirty-five hundred students. There is also an agricultural college. Another two thousand students attend universities in the United States, Great Britain, and other African countries.

Although this is a tremendous effort and a great improvement over the situation at independence, Botswana's schools are hard pressed to keep up with the country's birthrate. Even now, there are only enough spaces for three-fourths of the primary school graduates to move on to secondary school. Until 1988 secondary schools charged a tuition fee. Now these schools are free, as is university training. Some students who study abroad are supported by the government, although some receive scholarships from foreign countries. But there is not enough funding for the many students who would like to go abroad to study.

Botswana has its own school dropout problem. In the past when more families owned cattle, boys would leave school and travel to distant cattle posts to take care of the family cattle. Today fewer families have cattle. Now it is more often the girls who drop out because they become pregnant. When space in school was harder to come by, these girls were just forgotten. Today the government encourages girls to return to school to complete their education after they have their babies.

OTHER EDUCATIONAL PROGRAMS

Apart from formal education, the Brigades movement started at the time of independence trains young people in vocational schools. Through an apprenticeship program, young unemployed people over the age of sixteen are trained in practical skills such as carpentry, auto mechanics, and the building trades. The guiding spirit behind the Brigades was Patrick van Rensburg, originally from South Africa.

Other technical and vocational schools are maintained in twenty-one centers around the country, with about twelve

Patrick van Rensburg teaches building skills (left) to the Batswana. A literacy class for adults (above)

hundred trainees enrolled. These include publicly supported institutes as well as those offered by private companies, which provide both basic education as well as training for specific industries.

Because a substantial number of adult Batswana never went to school before independence, there are now programs for adult literacy in all the districts of the country. The program has suffered from many difficulties, notably the effects of the drought that gave literacy a lower priority than simply finding enough food and water.

At every level the government encourages people to go to school—and to stay in school. Skilled people are needed to build the country and to be able to replace more of the foreign nationals who now hold many of the most skilled positions in Botswana.

HEALTH

Botswana has been actively committed to improving the health of its citizens. At independence, there were no Batswana among

Medical professionals at a rural clinic

its 35 doctors. Twenty-five years later there were 35 Batswana doctors among the 255 who served the country. Much primary health care is in the hands of nurses. There are about 1,500 nurses with varying levels of professional training working in the country.

Today 85 percent of the population is within reach of some kind of health service—hospitals, clinics, or health posts. A health post is simply a house located in a remote area that has a population of less than five hundred people. The post offers basic health services and first aid and is visited by mobile health teams. Although there are only fourteen general hospitals, the system is successful in reaching most of the people. Three of the hospitals are owned and operated by major mining firms and three by missions. The rest are government hospitals. The life expectancy of fifty-nine years is much better than in many African countries. The infant mortality rate—a measure of how well a country is doing in taking care of its health needs—is about forty deaths per one thousand births. This is about the best rate of all African countries.

Traditional healers are recognized by the Ministry of Health as having a role to play in primary health care. There are an estimated two thousand such traditional practitioners in the country, using a variety of methods including herbs and faith healing. Many of them work with modern health care providers and exchange information and ideas.

Many health issues that affect people in Botswana are related to the lack of clean drinking water. One program aims to protect the water supply by keeping cattle away from boreholes and digging new boreholes away from people's living areas. The government is committed to immunizing children against communicable diseases and to seeing that all the people, including those in the most rural areas, are instructed in nutrition, child care, and family planning.

One of the most serious health problems in Botswana is malaria, carried by mosquitoes. Once malaria gets into the body, the disease progresses so quickly that unless treated immediately, it can quickly be life threatening. A spraying program helps to keep down the spread of mosquitoes. But the precautions—drugs, insect repellents, and sleeping under a net—are often not available or are too expensive for people to use all the time. Tuberculosis is widespread and spreads quickly, especially among the San who have moved into small, crowded government villages. Diarrhea caused by drinking dirty water is common.

The government has been successful in its immunization program. More than 75 percent of the children receive measles and polio vaccines. But family planning is still at a low level. Only about 15 percent of women use some form of family planning. The average number of children born to each woman is more than six. The population is expected to double in the next twenty years. That means that all government programs will have to work twice as hard just to stay even with the increase.

One of the most important government programs concerns food distribution during times of drought. Even people in the most remote areas of the country are reached by these programs. This is especially important because malnutrition makes people more vulnerable to disease and can quickly lead to death in children.

CULTURE

Until recent times, Batswana had no written language, but they always had a rich oral tradition. It was traditional during great gatherings of the people for a praise sayer to tell of the great deeds of the chief in a praise poem, called a *maboko*. As people became literate in English and in Setswana, they began to create a written history and literature. One of the early writers and translators was Solomon Tshekisho Plaatje. He wrote books in Setswana and translated them into English. He also translated Shakespeare's *Julius Caesar* and *Comedy of Errors*. Leetile Raditladi, a nephew of Tshekedi Khama, was a union organizer who wrote for a colonial-era newspaper. He was also a novelist and a poet and translated Shakespeare's *Macbeth*.

K. T. Motsete, founder of Botswana's first major political party, the Bechuanaland People's party (BPP), composed the country's national anthem, "Fatshe La Rona," which means "Blessed Country" in Setswana.

Palm fronds are dyed with vegetable stains and used to make baskets in traditional patterns. Some baskets are watertight.

HANDICRAFTS

Botswana's baskets are among the finest in the world. They are made from the doum palm that grows in the north. The baskets are made by the Mbukushu, river San, and Babirwa people, some of the smallest ethnic groups in Botswana.

They take the palm fronds and use them for weaving, allowing the tree to continue to grow and make new fronds. Using a special coiled weaving technique, they work the palm into patterns. The patterns are intricate and tell a story to those who know the symbols they represent. The basket makers add color to the tan-colored fronds by dying them with vegetable stains. When the baskets become wet, the coiled material swells and becomes watertight. These baskets are used for storing grain and seeds, for

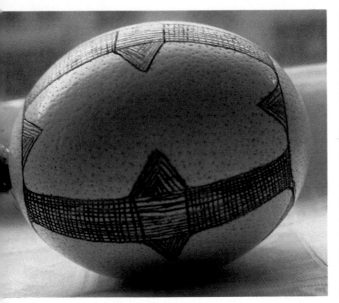

Ostrich eggshells (left) are decorated by the San and are also made into shell beads (right).

carrying water, and for serving homemade beer. Today they also are produced for sale to tourists, a way for the women to earn money.

In small workshops around Botswana, wood is used to make modern versions of the kgotla chair, the folding chair used in the village meetings. This is a particularly appropriate craft item because it represents one of Botswana's finest traditions.

In the National Museum and Art Gallery in Gaborone, artifacts may be seen that reflect traditional ways of life. These range from poison arrows to the finest examples of basket making. The museum holds exhibitions of contemporary work by painters, weavers, potters, sculptors, and photographers. For those who cannot travel to Gaborone, the museum has a mobile service that travels in a kind of safari van. Called *pitse-ya-naga*, meaning "zebra," because it is zebra striped, the vehicle brings exhibits to outlying regions.

Botswana also has its own National Library Service and a National Archives, as well as the University of Botswana Library. All of these contain publications about the country.

Scenes of Gaborone include a shopping area (top), spectators at a sporting event (above), and street vendors at the bus terminal (right).

Entrance to the mall in Gaborone

Chapter 7

THE CITIES

Botswana's cities reflect the concentration of activity along the rail lines, where most of the people live and where most of the business is located. The cities are growing at a rate of 7 percent a year, partly because of the persistent droughts that rob people of their farmlands and livestock and force them to look for paying work. It also reflects the growing number of Batswana who have some education and are looking for jobs. There are few nonagricultural jobs outside the cities and towns, other than at the mines and tourist areas.

GABORONE

Although Gaborone was made the capital of Botswana just a year before independence, there was a lively population here long before that. During the colonial period, starting about 1887, the village of Gaborone was established as a district headquarters. The name was that of the kgosi of the Batlokwa.

Since the capital city was built virtually from scratch in the 1960s, the city has a modern look. It is built around a broad central street called The Mall. Official buildings that house the

The Book Centre (above) an important book store and meeting place, and the President Hotel on the mall (right)

offices of the national and city governments are at either end of the mall. An estimated 140,000 people live in Gaborone, more than 10 percent of the country's population. The National Assembly and the National Museum and Art Gallery are housed here. The international airport is named for Sir Seretse Khama.

The Gaborone Dam, just outside the city, not only provides water for the inhabitants, but is also a popular park where people come to relax. When it was built, many thought the reservoir behind the dam would never fill with water because Botswana has so little rainfall. It was filled in three years, and continues to serve the capital well.

Francistown in the 1970s (above); local farmers bring produce (inset) to the market because the main road runs through Francistown.

FRANCISTOWN

In the northeast corner of Botswana, also along the rail line, is Francistown, the second-biggest city. This dusty town began as a trading post for the miners when gold was discovered in the 1870s, and it was named for an early prospector, Daniel Francis. Miners on their way to work the claims and returning with their earnings came through the railroad station at Francistown and spent much of their earnings here. Many trade unions began here in an effort to improve the living conditions of the mine workers. These later grew into some of Botswana's first political parties. Today, it is often the gathering place for tourists who are headed out on safari. It is also the site of Francistown Milling and Trading, which processes maize grown in Botswana into maize meal, a basic foodstuff.

An aerial view (above) of Maun and a close-up of a typical small grocery store there (inset)

MAUN

Maun, the safari capital of Botswana, and the traditional capital of the Batawana people, looks as if it has been created as a movie set for a Western. Its little airport has an endless parade of small aircraft during the height of the tourist season. Many Europeans make Maun their base while working on wildlife films and studies.

Serowe (above left) is the biggest traditional village in Africa.
The kgotla, meeting place (top right), and a statue of
Seretse Khama at his tomb (above right) in Serowe

SEROWE

Although still considered a village because of the way it is
structured, Serowe is the third-most populated area. As the chief
city of the Bangwato, it followed the layout of a traditional village
where the people live in simple round buildings, clustered around
a central meeting place. Newer construction is in a more modern
style. Serowe was the birthplace of Botswana's first president, Sir
Seretse Khama.

Tourists watch elephants from a safari vehicle (above), enjoy lunch in the patio of a restaurant (left), and talk near their sleeping tents (below) in Chobe National Park.

Chapter 8

THE LAST EDEN

TOURISM

Botswana is often called "the last Eden" because its wide open spaces and herds of elephants offer a look at the Africa of the past. The physical environment of Botswana is quite fragile and it is far from the usual safari route. The government has decided to pursue a specific kind of tourism. The idea is to bring in relatively few people, but focus on those who spend a great deal of money on their visits. The government has looked at other countries with large wildlife areas and found that large groups of people can be hard on the environment.

The government permits a limited amount of hunting in accordance with its policy of maintaining the herds at a reasonable size. Hunters pay a great deal of money for their licenses, and for having their "trophies" prepared and sent home. Recently the game park entrance fees were raised in a clear effort to discourage low-budget, high-volume tourism.

Botswana is an expensive destination. Not many people go there either for business or for tourism, so there are few flights. Most people who visit Botswana need a guide and a driver. Most roads in the wildlife areas are rough and require sturdy, four-wheel-drive vehicles and a knowledge of the terrain and the climate.

*The floodplain (above) of the Okavango Delta is fed by the
Okavango River and grows and diminishes with the rains.
As the water level drops, islands become larger (below).*

Botswana is not a place where visitors can easily jump into a rented car and take off on their own. About 100,000 tourists visit Botswana each year.

GAME RESERVES

About 17 percent of the land area has been designated as wildlife or nature reserves. Because there are relatively few visitors to Botswana, and because the game viewing areas are so vast, visitors are not likely to see many vehicles or other tourists. Game reserves are located in all but the eastern part of the country. The principal areas are the Central Kalahari Game Reserve, Gemsbok National Park in the extreme southwest corner, Chobe National Park in the north, Moremi Wildlife Reserve in the Okavango, and the Makgadikgadi Pan Game Reserve in the north central portion.

OKAVANGO

The Okavango Delta is a unique wild environment covering about 6,178 square miles (16,000 square kilometers), situated in the northwest section of Botswana. The delta is fed by the waters of the Okavango River, which grows and diminishes with the rains. Unlike most rivers, which flow to the sea, the Okavango spreads out onto the sands of the Kalahari Desert. Before it gets there, however, it creates the delta, an ever-changing mix of land and water, with little islands growing larger as the water level drops. With the return of the high waters following the rains, the islands become smaller, sometimes becoming completely submerged.

Visitors on the Okavango Delta are transported by canoe (above) to see sights such as the cape buffalo (right) in the Moremi Wildlife Reserve.

Within this mysterious place live many species of wildlife that thrive on the mix of grassland, marshland, and the river itself. Crocodiles are found in abundance. Birds feed on the wide variety of plant and insect life. Many kinds of fish live in the winding waterways. All around on the banks of the river are papyrus reeds and grasses. It is a mix of water and land unlike game reserves in other countries of Africa. The emphasis is on small camps set up on the larger islands. Visitors often reach their destinations and do much of their game viewing by boat, often in a dugout canoe called a *mokoro.*

A book about the Okavango, called *Sea of Land, Land of Water,* sums up the mysterious landscape of the region.

Moremi Wildlife Reserve lies within the Okavango Delta. (The delta itself is not a reserve.) In Moremi, there are forests of giant acacia trees and dense mopane woods. Cape buffalo, vast herds of

Elephants (above), in the Moremi Wildlife Reserve, and hippopotamuses (inset)

elephants, giraffes, and beautiful antelopes called *kudu* all live here.

Some parts of the delta are covered with water throughout the year. In other parts the waters ebb and flow like a great inland tide. With all the water coming and going, the animals are always coming and going too, on migrations that cover vast distances. Elephants, cape buffalo, zebras, and wildebeests follow ancient routes in and out of the delta, as well as in dry parts of the Kalahari itself, to the south of the delta.

Often, the animals move toward a region because they can sense the rains are coming. Hippos, which must have permanent sources of water to live in, stay within the range of the river, feeding on its grasses. Many species of antelope live within the grassy areas. They have adapted to the specific types of reeds and grass they find growing there.

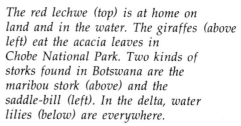

The red lechwe (top) is at home on land and in the water. The giraffes (above left) eat the acacia leaves in Chobe National Park. Two kinds of storks found in Botswana are the maribou stork (above) and the saddle-bill (left). In the delta, water lilies (below) are everywhere.

FENCES AND MIGRATIONS

Some of the migration routes have been disrupted by the government. Starting in the 1950s, fences, stretching over great distances, were built to separate the wildlife from the herds of cattle, to protect the cattle from disease. These precautions make it possible for commercial herds to meet standards set by countries that import the beef. But when the wildlife cannot complete their migration, they die. In bad years, when water is scarce, they die along the fences by the tens of thousands.

BIRD LIFE

The bird life is busy when the waters are highest. The brilliantly colored malachite kingfisher comes to snatch fish out of the water. Maribou storks and saddle-bill storks come to build their nests and have their young while food is abundant.

Insects spring to life at this time, providing the birds with a variety of food. Mosquitoes and dragonflies are everywhere. They are the favorite prey for the reed frogs. The frogs eat the insects, the large birds eat the frogs, and sometimes spiders eat the fish. The red lechwe, an antelope that is as much at home in the water as it is on land, lives on the delta's floodplain. Impala and tsessebe are two other antelopes found here.

The delta comes alive with flowers, too. Water lilies are everywhere, turning the delta into a huge lily pond. Papyrus reeds grow straight out of the water. Along the shore, on the islands, grow knob thorn acacia trees, palm trees, and strangler fig trees, named for the thick vinelike sections that wrap themselves around the trunk.

It is not only the seasonal rains that change the look and shape of the Okavango Delta. The frequent changes in the amount of water force the land to shift, and sometimes these shifts are quite violent. In the process, some new channels are created and others are closed off. In years past, the Okavango and Chobe rivers were often connected by a spillway that carried the overflow of the Okavango into the Chobe. But extremely dry conditions over the past decade have nearly put an end to this. If the region continues to experience severe droughts, it is likely that these two systems will become totally separate.

In the Okavango, a vigorous spraying program against the tsetse fly may soon kill off these disease-carrying insects that affect cattle. It is feared that then the government will agree to open the grassy areas of the Okavango to cattle growers and that could spell the end to the delicate balance of the region.

ELEPHANT WALKS

African elephants are different from Indian elephants. They are larger, and both the female and the male have tusks. African elephants are thought to be unsuitable for the kinds of chores that are taught to Asian elephants. Yet in a tiny corner of Botswana, a visitor can ride on the back of an elephant—a remarkable way to see the terrain. This group of elephants had a strange safari of their own. Originally from South Africa, they were brought to the United States and trained for a circus. When the circus failed, the animals were to be sent back to Africa. Because of the sanctions then in place against South Africa, the elephants couldn't go there so they wound up in Botswana! The whole family came back, including the smallest ones.

Lions climb trees in Chobe National Park.

Map legend:
- Central Kalahari Game Reserve
- Gemsbok National Park
- Chobe National Park
- Moremi Wildlife Reserve
- Makgadikgadi Pan Game Reserve
- Nxai Pan National Park

Gaborone

CHOBE NATIONAL PARK

Next to the Okavango, embracing the floodplains of the Chobe River, is the Chobe National Park. It lies just sixty-two miles (one hundred kilometers) southwest of Victoria Falls. The sanctuary is part of the Batawana people's tribal land. It was created in 1962, before Botswana gained its independence, to protect it from too much hunting. Chobe is known for its elephants, said to be the largest herd remaining in Africa. Here, too, is the Savuti Channel, which dried out completely in the nineteenth century and then, without explanation, began to fill up again in 1957. It is home to many of the largest species of game including giraffes, cape buffalo, lions, hippos, and wildebeests. Lions climb trees in Chobe National Park, one of the few places in Africa where they do that.

When David Livingstone traveled along Chobe's channels in a mokoro in 1851, he described the beauty and expanse of the river

103

A mother elephant stands patiently while her baby nurses.

and the vegetation. Today, though the herds are greatly reduced in size, the visitor can still experience much of the wildness that struck Livingstone as he made his way along the river channels. Chobe is a bird-watcher's paradise; as many as 450 species have been spotted here.

Here in the vast areas of the north poachers kill about one hundred to two hundred elephants a year. But Botswana's elephant problem is an unusual one in Africa these days. It is one of the few countries where elephants are increasing rapidly. An estimated sixty thousand elephants live in Botswana. With their huge appetites, this number is thought to be too many for the land to sustain. A decision may be made soon to begin reducing the herds by killing selected family groups. Because elephants are such social creatures, and have a strong family life, it is much kinder to kill an entire family rather than just take out the reproductive female or bull and leave the rest of the herd grieving

Zebras, as well as other animals, migrate to find water.

for them. The abundance of elephants points up the benefit of tourism, as opposed to mining. Wildlife is a renewable resource if it is protected.

THE PANS

Nxai Pan National Park and Makgadikgadi Game Reserve were created around the natural phenomenon of a pan. Pans are lakes that have dried up. This shallow depression is found on an open flatland. When it rains, the pan fills with water. Though shallow, water-filled pans attract a great deal of game—sometimes as many as two thousand zebras may be found in an area, as well as many species of birds. As the pans dry up, the animals become even more concentrated, competing for the remaining water. Travel by tourists to these regions is usually timed to coincide with the end of the rainy season, when the pans are full, and the roads are reasonably passable.

A San village in the Kalahari Desert

CENTRAL KALAHARI GAME RESERVE

The Central Kalahari Game Reserve was set aside in 1961, not as a game park but as a place where the San people could live their traditional life of hunting and gathering. There is a great deal of game in this huge 20,000-square-mile (51,800-square-kilometer) region, which has no surface water source at all. But cattle frequently graze in it, which has made it very difficult for the San people to live here. The problem of balancing the needs of cattle owners, the needs of the wildlife, and the life of the San people has yet to be resolved.

ADDITIONAL SET-ASIDE LANDS

In addition to the 17 percent of the land set aside as wildlife reserves, another 22 percent is slated to be devoted to wildlife management. This program, called Wildlife Management Areas, is designed to allow tourism and hunting to exist alongside the local people's use of the land for grazing.

Chapter 9

MANY ROLES TO PLAY

BOTSWANA AND THE WORLD

Though landlocked, suffering periodic droughts, and unable to grow enough food, Botswana still stands out in Africa as an example of how an independent country can nurture its citizens and make the most of its resources. It is often called the most democratic country in Africa, stemming from the kgotla tradition and the remarkable, intelligent rule of its two presidents. Botswana had a stable transition of power on the death of Sir Seretse and has had regular, peaceful elections, as established in the constitution since independence. It has never had a civil war, an attempt to overthrow the government, or riots. It has not been plagued by corruption, which saps the economy of many African states. On Botswana's flag there are two broad bands of blue that represent the blue sky and the blue water of the Okavango Delta. The blue bands are flanked by two narrow strips of white and one wider band of black, representing the different racial groups within the society.

BOTSWANA AND SOUTH AFRICA

Botswana's relationship with South Africa has never been one of equals. Before independence the people feared becoming part of

South Africa. After independence, South Africa's overwhelming control of Botswana's economy became a source of great discomfort. South Africa's mines employ a significant portion of Botswana's labor force. South Africa's industrial output makes it uneconomical for Botswana to set up factories to make most of the manufactured products and foodstuffs it needs. Botswana depends on South Africa for the transport of 85 percent of its imports. These include products made in South Africa as well as those made elsewhere, because Botswana has no direct outlet to seaports. Even Botswana's beef, destined for Europe, must be exported through South Africa. Botswana's most valuable commodity—diamonds—can be taken out by air since they weigh so little.

The most aggressive actions by South Africa were focused on rooting out the members of the African National Congress (ANC) who had taken refuge in Botswana. Botswana never turned its back on those struggling for equality in South Africa, although it never allowed training camps or weapons on its territory. But South Africa did not concern itself with these distinctions and went after the ANC fighters near their common border—often with the loss of innocent lives. The most blatant example was a long predawn raid on ten houses scattered around Gaborone in 1985, during which at least fifteen people were killed.

Dramatic changes began to take place in South Africa when its president, F. W. de Klerk, released Nelson Mandela from prison, allowed formerly banned political groups to organize and hold meetings, and announced that apartheid policies were no longer the law of the land. As soon as a government is put into place in South Africa, with the majority black population included, diplomatic relations between Botswana and South Africa can be

Left: President F.W. de Klerk of South Africa and his wife
Right: President Masire listens to Nelson Mandela speak in Gaborone in the 1990s.

established. When a nonracial government is elected in South Africa, Botswana should benefit greatly from having a powerful and friendly neighbor. In the meantime, it has increased its defense spending. It is building up its defense forces, now numbering more than six thousand, even while acknowledging that they would never be a match for South Africa's massive, well-trained, well-equipped force. And it means that money needed for basic human services must be diverted to such facilities as a new air base, west of Gaborone.

BOTSWANA AND GREAT BRITAIN

Although Great Britain's attitude toward Seretse Khama was one of outright hostility, when Botswana became independent Khama reached out a hand of friendship and accepted a place in the British Commonwealth of Nations. This "club" is a loosely knit group of former colonies, protectorates, and other British possessions that have gained their independence. The countries that are part of this association contain about one-quarter of the entire world's population, now more than one billion people. The

Norman Rush (left) chats with a book buyer

Commonwealth nations gather every two years in one of the member states. By joining together, small countries such as Botswana gain the strength of the whole group. Great Britain has been generous with aid to Botswana, especially during the years before income began to flow from the new diamond mines.

BOTSWANA AND THE UNITED STATES

The United States actively applauds Botswana's democratic traditions and supports it with a variety of programs. It has one of the biggest Peace Corps forces anywhere, with about 160 to 200 volunteers at work in Botswana, helping mainly in education. Over the years since independence, more than 1,600 American Peace Corps workers have played their part in helping Botswana's people. In addition to education, many work to improve water distribution, work on economic planning, and promote small business development and public health programs. Norman Rush and his wife Else were co-directors of the Peace Corps in Botswana for five years. His stay there inspired him to write the novel *Mating* and a collection of short stories called *Whites*. The land and its people are important parts of his writing.

United States aid to Botswana has focused on education, too. It supports programs in Botswana and funds more than eight

Fences are used to control migration of animals.

hundred Batswana in college programs in the United States. The
Voice of America radio program has a relay station in Botswana,
the only one in southern Africa, and serves the whole region. The
United States has provided assistance in military training for the
Botswana Defense Force, as well as direct economic aid to the
country. U.S. armed forces conduct training exercises here, getting
experience in a rough terrain that has no equal at home.

American citizens, on their own, have traveled to Botswana,
contributing their energy and education. One of the best-known
examples is Mark and Delia Owens, an American couple who
lived in the Kalahari under the harshest conditions for seven
years studying desert lions and brown hyenas. During that time,
they observed at first hand the government's policy of fencing and
its impact on wildlife. They made suggestions about managing the
wildlife and the land. Their ideas were controversial, and
ultimately they had to leave the country.

SOUTHERN AFRICAN CUSTOMS UNION

Botswana is a member of the Southern African Customs Union (SACU), along with Lesotho, Swaziland, and South Africa. Most goods are not assessed any kind of duty when they travel between any of these countries. In addition, South Africa collects the duties due to the countries from other sources and pays out a share to each country. This gives Botswana about 15 percent of its yearly revenue. At independence, Botswana used South Africa's currency, the rand. In 1976 Botswana issued its own currency, called the pula.

Botswana is also a member of the Lome Convention. This is an agreement between developing countries and the members of the European Community that allows duty-free access to the huge European market.

SADC

Botswana was one of the ten-member states of the Southern African Development Coordination Conference (SADCC), a group whose main aim was to find ways to become less dependent on South Africa for transport, markets, and technology. SADCC was headquartered in Gaborone. After the announced changes in South Africa in 1990, the group changed its name to Southern African Development Community (SADC) and expects South Africa to become a member some time in the future. Cooperation with a "new" South Africa will be much more beneficial to the smaller economies neighboring it than trying to find ways to compete against it. SADC is headquartered in Gaborone.

The future looks promising for these schoolgirls of Gaborone.

WHAT DOES THE FUTURE HOLD?

In spite of the many difficult conditions that may lie in the future for the people of Botswana, the country has a good chance for success. It has one of the rarest of all commodities in Africa— fine leadership. The president and other officials have followed the long tradition of taking good care—of choosing well for the people. They have resisted wasting the income from their natural resources. Now as South Africa proceeds with its own movement toward complete democracy and with prospects for peace improving in the whole region, Botswana can concentrate on developing its industrial base, improving its educational system, and finding ways to make daily life better for all the people.

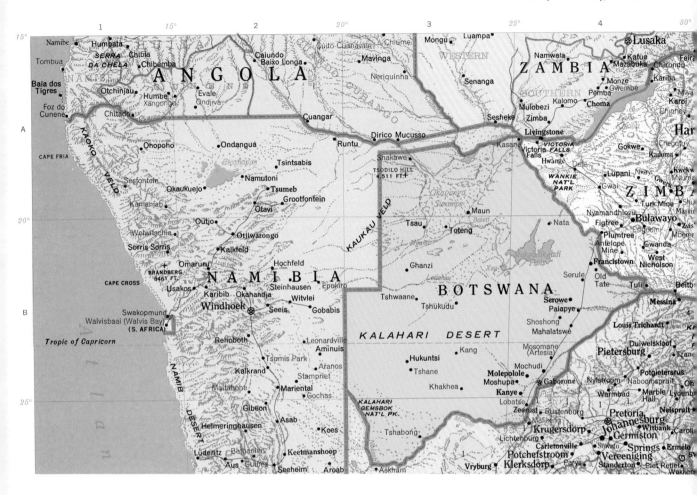

MAP KEY

		Lake Ngandi	B3	Palapye	B4	
		Letiahau (river)	B3	Serowe	B4	
Boteti (river)	B3	Lobatse	C4	Serule	B4	
Chobe (river)	A3	Mahalatswe	B4	Shakawe	A3	
Francistown	B4	Makgadikgadi Pans (plains)	B4	Shashi (river)	B4	
Gaborone	B4	Maun	A3	Shoshong	B4	
Ghanzi	B3	Mochudi	B4	Toteng	B3	
Hukuntsi	B3	Molepolole	B4	Tsau	B3	
Kalahari Desert	B3, B4	Molopo (river)	C3, C4	Tshabong	C3	
Kalahari Gemsbok National Park	C3	Moshupa	B4	Tshane	B3	
Kang	B3	Mosomane (Artesia)	B4	Tshukudu	B3	
Kanye	B4	Nata	B4	Tshwaane	B3	
Kassane	A4	Nossob (river)	C3	Tsodilo Hills (mountains)	A3	
Kaukau Veld (mountain range)	A3, B3	Okavango Swamps	A3, B3	Tule	B4	
Khakhea	B3	Old Tate	B4	Xau (lake)	B3	

Opposite page: A water hole at sundown

MINI-FACTS AT A GLANCE

GENERAL INFORMATION

Official Name: Republic of Botswana (formerly Bechuanaland)

Capital: Gaborone

Government: Botswana is a multiparty republic. The 35-member National Assembly elects the president for a five-year term. The president is the head of state and government and appoints a cabinet, which is responsible to the National Assembly. Leaders of the nation's major ethnic groups make up the House of Chiefs that advises the government on ethnic issues. Botswana is one of the few African countries with more than one political party. It is often called the most democratic country in Africa. Administratively the country is divided into ten districts.

Religion: There is no official religion, but the constitution guarantees freedom of religion to all. Traditional African beliefs are very strong; some one-half of the population follows traditional beliefs. Christianity is the second-largest religion, with Protestants 29 percent and Roman Catholics 10 percent; other religions make up 11 percent.

Ethnic Composition: Tswana is the largest ethnic group with some three-fourths of the total population. The Tswana are divided into eight major groups; most of them live in the eastern part except the Batswana who live in the northwest area known as Ngamiland. The San (also called Bushmen of the Kalahari) have been living in Botswana for as long as 50 thousand years. Some 15 thousand whites also live in Botswana. About two million Tswana from the Barolong group live in Bophuthatswana in South Africa.

Language: English and Setswana are the official languages; most of the people speak Setswana.

National Flag: Five horizontal stripes of varying widths are displayed on the national flag. Light blue top and bottom stripes are separated from a smaller black middle stripe by two thin white stripes. The black and white stripes emphasize. Botswana's commitment to racial equality; the pale blue stripes symbolize the blue sky and blue water of the Okavango Delta.

National Anthem: *Fatshe La Rona* ("Blessed Country")

Money: The pula (P), containing 100 thebes, is the national currency. In 1993, 1 Botswana pula was equal to almost $0.50 in United States currency.

Weights and Measures: The metric system is in use.

Population: 1,320,000 (1991 census); distribution 24 percent urban and 76 percent rural; density 5.9 persons per sq. mi. (2.3 persons per sq km)

Cities:

Gaborone	133,791 (1991 census)
Francistown	65,026 (1991 census)
Selebi-Pikwe	39,769 (1991 census)
Molepolole	29,212 (1988 estimate)
Serowe	28,267 (1988 estimate)

GEOGRAPHY

Highest Point: Otse Mountain, 4,886 ft. (1,489 m)

Lowest Point: Near the junction of the Shashe and Limpopo rivers, 1,684 ft. (513 m)

Rivers and lakes: There is very little permanent surface water in Botswana. The Chobe, Limpopo, Nossob, Okavango, and Shashi are the principal rivers, but during dry periods, most of the rivers dry up completely.

The Okavango Delta in the north, covering about 3 percent of the total land area, is an inland marshy delta—the largest such in the world. The Okavango River water spreads over the land, and gradually all of this water evaporates. Only half of the delta is covered with water throughout the year. Crocodiles are in abundance, and mosquitoes, dragonflies, reed frogs, spiders, red lechwes, impalas, lions, giraffes, hippos, and tsessebe antelopes inhabit the Okavango Delta.

Lake Ngami is rarely filled with water. The Makgadikgadi Pan is a huge salt lake in the east that receives water only during seasons of exceptionally heavy rainfall; it dries quickly, leaving the land covered with a residue of salt. Pans are lakes that have dried up; when it rains, the pan fills with water. Underground wells provide some drinking water.

Wildlife: Five game reserves, three game sanctuaries, and 40 controlled hunting areas make up some 17 percent of the land of Botswana. Wildlife includes lions, leopards, cheetahs, elephants, giraffes, zebras, hippopotamuses, rhinoceroses, duikers, cape buffalo, hyenas, and several varieties of antelope. Some 400 birds are indigenous to Botswana, including the brilliantly colored malachite kingfisher, fish eagle, maribou storks, and saddle-bill storks. Tsetse (a disease carrying fly), which lives on wildlife, makes these areas dangerous for cattle.

The government permits a limited amount of hunting; hunters pay a great deal of money for their licenses. The major game reserves are the Central Kalahari Game Reserve, Chobe National Park, Gemsbok National Park, Makgadikgadi Pan Game Reserve, Moremi Wildlife Reserve, and Nxai Pan National Park. Chobe National Park has the largest herd of elephants remaining in Africa; poachers kill about one hundred to two hundred elephants a year in Chobe alone. The government has been building great stretches of fences to separate the wildlife from the herds of domestic cattle.

Climate: January is the hottest month of the year and July the coldest. Most of the country is hot throughout the year; cooler temperatures prevail in the higher altitudes. Summer lasts from October to April; daytime temperatures can reach 100° F. (38° C). Heavy frost can occur in the night during winter months especially in the south. Rainfall has become more and more uncertain over the last few decades. Average annual rainfall is about 18 in. (45 cm), ranging from 27 in. (69 cm) in the north to less than 10 in. (25 cm) in the Kalahari Desert. Droughts are frequent; a severe drought across all southern Africa in the early 1980s and again in the early 1990s, killed crops and livestock.

Greatest Distance: North to South: 625 mi. (1,006 km)
East to West: 590 mi. (950 km)

Area: 231,805 sq. mi. (600,376 sq km)

ECONOMY AND INDUSTRY

Agriculture: Less than 2.5 percent of the land is under agriculture and permanent cultivation. Rainfall determines most of the agricultural activities, as irrigation is available only in small areas near the Chobe and Limpopo rivers, for commercial farming. Major crops are sorghum, corn, millet, melons, pulses (peas or beans), onions, oranges, seed cotton, and peanuts.

Cattle are considered wealth and a source of status by Tswana people. About 75 percent of the land is under some kind of pasture for livestock; beef production is the single-largest agricultural activity. In good rain years, the national herd can grow as large as three million head of cattle. Botswana has three large *abattoirs,* slaughterhouses. Some 90 percent of the beef is exported, largely to European countries. The beef exporting business is in the hands of a few commercial ranchers. The cattle are moved annually through the bush to marketplaces or to slaughterhouses. Other domestic animals include goats, sheep, donkeys, and horses; chickens are kept for their eggs and also to eat.

Mining: The mining sector is dominated by diamond production. Some 14 million carats of diamonds, mostly of industrial quality, are produced every year. Botswana is the largest producer of gem diamonds in the world. Orapa, Letlhakane, and Jwaneng are the three largest diamond mines. Botswana has reserves of soda ash, nickel, copper, salt, plutonium, asbestos, chromite, fluorspar, iron, manganese, potash, silver, talc, and uranium. Coal and gold are also mined.

Manufacturing: Manufacturing is limited to food products, beverages, textiles, small machinery, metal products, shoes, garments, chemicals, and paper products. Diamond-cutting factories are training local people. There is a soda ash plant at Sua Pan and a copper and nickel smelter at Selebi-Phikwe.

Transportation: Air Botswana is the national airline. Sir Seretse Khama International Airport is at Gaborone. There are seven other airports with scheduled flights. Botswana has only about 443 mi. (713 km) of railway tracks. Total road length is about 9,942 mi. (16,000 km), of which some 15 percent is paved. A major road connects Lobatse in the south to Gaborone and Francistown in the north.

Communication: There is one government-operated radio station. Although there is no Botswana television service, some private clubs arrange to receive TV signals from South Africa and BopTV from Bophuthatswana. There is one government newspaper, the *Daily News* with some 37,000 circulation, and a number of privately printed weekly newspapers. Telephone service is available in the major cities and some rural areas. A new telephone system, installed in 1986, permits international direct dialing to countries around the world, but not to the neighboring countries.

Trade: Major import items are transport equipment, machinery, electrical goods, food and tobacco items, chemicals, rubber, metal products, textiles, footwear, petroleum, and wood and paper products. Major import sources are South Africa, Lesotho, Namibia, Swaziland, Great Britain, and the United States. Chief export items are diamonds, copper, nickel, and meat products; diamonds alone account for almost 75 percent of the total exports. Chief export destinations are Great Britain, Swaziland, South Africa, Lesotho, Namibia, and the United States.

EVERYDAY LIFE

Health: The health care system is presently small but is constantly being extended. Apart from some 14 general hospitals and a mental hospital, primary health care in rural areas is provided by health clinics, health posts, and mobile health stops.

Education: Some 73 percent of the population can read and write. Education is not compulsory by law but is provided free of charge up to university training. Primary education begins at seven years of age and lasts for seven years. Secondary education begins at the age of 14 and lasts for another five years. There are very few secondary schools; only one-fifth of all children attending elementary school go on to high school. For the first four years children are taught in Setswana; then English is used. The University of Botswana is in Gaborone. There are several vocational schools, agricultural colleges, and teacher-training colleges. Many students attend universities in the United States, Great Britain, and other African countries. A semi-autonomous unit called the Brigade provides vocational training in carpentry, auto mechanics, and construction. The government provides adult education programs in all districts of the country. About one-fifth of the nation's budget is spent on education.

Holidays:

New Year's Day, January 1
Good Friday, Friday before Easter
Easter, (variable)
Ascension Day, (forty days after Easter)
President's Day, July 15-16
Botswana Day, September 30 to October 1
Christmas, December 25
Boxing Day, December 26

Culture: A praise poem called a *maboko* tells the great deeds of the chiefs of the past. Botswana's baskets are among the finest in the world. Made from the daum palm, these baskets are used for storing grain seed, for carrying water, and for serving homemade beer. Folding kgotla wooden chairs, used in village meetings, are another fine example of handicrafts.

The thirty-five hundred historic rock paintings at the Tsodilo Hills are about two to three thousand years old. The National Museum, the National Archives, and the Art Gallery at Gaborone have fine examples of the Botswana way of life. The National Museum has a mobile service that travels from village to village. Botswana has a National Library Service.

Housing: Traditional round homes are called *rondavels*; they are grouped

119

together as part of a large village. Houses are made of clay and then covered with a mixture of mud. They are often made of concrete today. The roof is generally made of thatch. All members of a family live close together in a village. People have a second home near the fields where they tend to crops, sometimes for several months at a stretch. Families with cattle have a third home near the cattle post, or *moraka*, sometimes miles away from the first home.

Food: Corn or sorghum porridge is the basic food of most of the people. Cooking is done on an open fire and the usual fuel is wood. Batswana traditionally supplemented their diet with meat from hunting and gathering foods. The San once lived as hunter gatherers; they make use of all nuts, fruits, wild melons, roots, and leaves found growing in the Kalahari. Today they survive by a mixed economy.

Recreation: Soccer is a major form of recreation for boys and young men and is played throughout the country. Discos and movies and other events are held at community centers, bars, and hotels. The Gaborone Dam provides a popular park for recreation.

IMPORTANT DATES

?-1000 B.C.—Rock paintings are carved in Tsodilo Hills

A.D. 01-1000—San living in present-day Botswana are pushed into the Kalahari Desert by the Tswana

1200s—Negroid people called Bantu, including the Tswana, move south out of Central Africa and settle in the area south of the Limpopo River

1700s—Tswana move into Botswana area

1811—William Burchell travels to Botswana region to study the wildlife and the terrain

1815—The first missionary school is started by Robert Moffat

1836—Cornwallis Harris reaches the Botswana region

1849—David Livingstone reaches Lake Ngami

1851—Livingstone travels along the Chobe River channels

1861—Central Kalahari Game Reserve is established

1867—Gold is discovered in the Tati region

1872—Khama III is chief of Ngwato

1880—Boers (farmers of Dutch origin) and the British fight a war that ends in British defeat

1885—Bechuanaland Protectorate is established

1887 — The village of Gaborone is established as the district headquarters

1889 — British Bechuanaland is incorporated into the Cape Colony

1895 — Three principal *dikgosi* — Khama III, Sebele, and Bathoen — travel to England to meet Joseph Chamberlain

1895 — A disease called *rinderpest* strikes the nation's cattle; it kills more than 90 percent of the cattle in the protectorate

1899 — The protectorate land is divided up into reserves for different clans

1899-1902 — The Boer War takes place in southern Africa

1904 — Germans kill many Herero people in Namibia; many Herero flee to Botswana

1905 — A veterinary government department is opened

1922 — British set up an Advisory Council, originally called the Native Advisory Council; it is renamed the African Advisory Council in 1940

1923 — Isang Pilane builds the Mochudi National School

1925 — Tshekedi Khama becomes the acting head of the Bangwato

1930 — Charles Rey is installed as the British resident commissioner

1932 — The first school above the primary level is opened for Africans in the protectorate; the British present a proclamation to the *dikgosi*

1934 — British proclamations that greatly reduce the independence of Batswana people become law

1937 — Charles Arden-Clarke replaces Charles Rey as the British resident commissioner

1942 — Ten thousand Batswana leave to fight in World War II

1943 — New proclamations are issued by the British that are more acceptable

1947 — South Africa appeals to the United Nations for incorporation of Southwest Africa into the Union of South Africa as its fifth province; the request is denied

1948 — The official policy of *apartheid* is instituted in South Africa; Seretse Khama marries a white Englishwoman in England

1954 — The first *abattoir*, cattle slaughterhouse, is opened at Lobatse; presently it is the largest in Africa

1956 — Sir Seretse is permitted to come home from exile in England; geologists find three diamonds in a riverbed

1960—Bechuanaland Protectorate Legislative Council is established

1962—Chobe National Park is created

1965—Elections are held; Bechuanaland Democratic party (BDP) receives 80 percent of the total vote

1966—Republic of Botswana is proclaimed with Sir Seretse Khama as its first president; official flag is adopted; government-run radio station, Radio Botswana, starts broadcasting in both English and Setswana

1967—Diamonds are discovered in commercial quantity

1969—A new customs agreement is signed with South Africa; general elections are held

1971—The first national population census is taken

1974—Sir Seretse is reelected president

1976—The pula (p) is introduced as the new national currency, replacing the South African rand (R)

1977—Relations with Rhodesia (present-day Zimbabwe) are strained over an armed border conflict; an all-weather road from southern Botswana to Zambia is completed; South Africa declares Bophuthatswana independent (no other country in the world recognizes it)

1979—Sir Seretse is reelected president

1980—President Seretse dies of cancer; he is succeeded by Vice-President Sir Quett Masire; the Sun City entertainment complex opens in Bophuthatswana

1982—The Savuti River dries up completely; the Jwaneng diamond mine starts production

1983—Botswana and Zimbabwe establish full diplomatic relations

1984—General elections are held; Sir Masire is reelected president

1985—South African forces raid ten houses in Gaborone looking for members of the African National Congress (ANC)

1986—A modern telephone system is introduced

1987—Botswana and Mozambique establish a permanent joint commission; De Beers purchases Botswana's stockpile of diamonds; the government takes control of the Zimbabwe Railways

1989—Botswana Democratic party wins the national elections

1990—Some 10 percent of all salaried workers are employed in South Africa; South Africa announces that apartheid policies are no longer the law of the land;

the Botswana government frees 16 members of South African liberation movements

1991—Botswana leaders attend the first summit of Africans and African-Americans in Abidjan, Ivory Coast; the Seventh National Development Plan begins

1992—Some 30 thousand households are equipped with electricity

IMPORTANT PEOPLE

Charles Arden-Clarke, British resident commissioner in Bechuanaland Protectorate in the 1930s

William Burchell (1781?-1863), a naturalist; perhaps the first white man to travel in the Botswana region; he worked on a Tswana dictionary in the 1810s

Martin Chakaliso, launched a new political party, the Botswana Liberal party in 1983

Joseph Chamberlain (1836-1914), British politician; British colonial secretary from 1895 to 1903

Daniel Francis, an early prospector; Francistown is named after him

Cornwallis Harris, a naturalist; published accounts of his adventures in the 1830s of the Kalahari region

Rasebolai Kgamanee, kgosi chosen by the British to replace Tshekedi Khama

Sir Seretse Khama (1821-80), Botswana's first president; leader of the Bechuanaland Democratic party (BDP); president from 1969 to 1980; a knight of the British Empire

Tshekedi Khama (1905-59), head of the Bangwato from 1925 to 1950; uncle of Sir Seretse Khama; exiled by British in 1950

Khama III (1837-1923), king (1875-1923); leader of the Bangwato; converted to Christianity in 1860; grandfather of Sir Seretse Khama

Richard Lee (1937-   ), an anthropologist who works with the San

David Livingstone (1813-1873), Scottish missionary, author, and explorer; discovered Lake Ngami in 1849, Zambezi River in 1851, Victoria Falls in 1855, Lake Nyasa in 1859, and Lake Mweru in 1867; known for his explorations in south central Africa

Nelson Mandela (1918-   ), South African lawyer and African National Congress leader, convicted and sentenced to life for treason in 1964, he was released in 1990

Lucas Mangope, president of Bophuthatswana

John Marshall (1932-   ), an American filmmaker; his film *The Hunters* (among many others) depicts the way of life of San people; started the Ju/Wa Development Foundation in Namibia, with Megan Biesele, to help the San

Lorna Marshall, author of the first contemporary anthropological writings on the San

Sir Quett Masire (1925-   ), succeeded Sir Seretse as president in 1980; reelected president in 1984; made a knight of the British Empire; won the leadership award from the Hunger Project US in 1989

Peter Mmusi (1929-   ), vice-president, since 1983

Mary Moffat (?-1862), daughter of Robert Moffat; married David Livingstone in 1844

Robert Moffat (1795-1883), Scottish missionary; father of Mary Moffat and father-in-law of David Livingstone; translated the New Testament into Tswana in 1839 and the Old Testament in 1857

S.M. Molema, historian of the Batswana

K.T. Motsete (1899-1975), founded Botswana's first major political party, Bechuanaland People's party (BPP), composed country's national anthem

Cotton Oswell, led the exploration team of David Livingstone to Lake Ngami

Mark and Delia Owens, American citizens and naturalists; lived for seven years in Kalahari region studying desert lions and brown hyenas

Isang Pilane, leader of the Bakgatla, ruled from 1921 to 1929; in 1923 he built a huge school for his people to learn English, mathematics, and other modern skills

Solomon Tshekisho Plaatje (1875-1932), writer; wrote books in Setswana, such as *Native Life in South Africa*, and then translated them into English; also translated some of Shakespeare's works into Setswana

Laurens van der Post, novelist; wrote account of San in *The Lost World of the Kalahari* and *A Story Like the Wind*

Leetile Raditladi (1910-71), a nephew of Tshekedi Khama; union organizer, writer, and poet

Charles Rey (1877-1968), British resident commissioner in Bechuanaland Protectorate in the 1930s

Cecil John Rhodes (1853-1902), British colonial administrator and financier; owner of the British South Africa Company (BSAC); built railroads and created a mining empire in southern Africa; the former country of Rhodesia (now Zimbabwe) was named after him; established by will a scholarship in his name for education at Oxford University in England

Patrick van Rensburg, South African who started the Brigade movement to teach vocational skills to youths in Botswana

Sebele II, a Bakwena leader who ruled from 1918 to 1939; jailed by the British without a trial; spent last eight years of his life as a political prisoner

Seepapitso II (1884-1916), tribal leader, ruled from 1910 to 1916; created a written record of his rule; constructed schools, dams, and tried to improve local living conditions

Sekgoma Khama II (?-1925), leader of the Bangwato

Shaka (1787?-1828), a fierce Zulu leader

Elizabeth Marshall Thomas (1931-   ), sister of John Marshall; wrote a popular account of the !Kung, *The Harmless People*

Jamie Uys, South African filmmaker; made *The Gods Must Be Crazy*

Ruth Williams, an Englishwoman; married Sir Seretse Khama in England in 1948

INDEX

Page numbers that appear in boldface type indicate illustrations

About the Author

Jason Lauré was born in Chehalis, Washington, and lived in California before joining the United States army and serving in France. He attended Columbia University and worked for *The New York Times*. He traveled to San Francisco and became a photographer during the turbulent 1960s. He recorded those events before setting out on the first of many trips to foreign countries that were experiencing their own turmoil.

Mr. Lauré has written Enchantment of the World books on Zimbabwe, Zambia, Angola, Bangladesh, and Namibia.

Mr. Lauré is now based in South Africa, where he is covering the transition to a democratic government and working on a documentary about the dramatic changes in that country.

Mr. Lauré is married to Marisia Lauré, a native of Angola, who is a Portuguese language translator and interpreter.